The Four Pillars of Politics

Lexington Studies in Political Communication
Series Editor: Robert E. Denton, Jr., Virginia Polytechnic Institute and State University

This series encourages focused work examining the role and function of communication in the realm of politics including campaigns and elections, media, and political institutions.

The Four Pillars of Politics

Why Some Candidates Don't Win and Other's Can't Lead

James T. Kitchens and Larry Powell

LEXINGTON BOOKS
Lanham • Boulder • New York • London

2/6/18
LB
$ 39.99

Published by Lexington Books
An imprint of The Rowman & Littlefield Publishing Group, Inc.
4501 Forbes Boulevard, Suite 200, Lanham, Maryland 20706
www.rowman.com

Unit A, Whitacre Mews, 26-34 Stannary Street, London SE11 4AB

British Library Cataloguing in Publication Information Available

Library of Congress Cataloging-in-Publication Data
Kitchens, James T.
The four pillars of politics : why some candidates don't win and others can't lead / James T. Kitchens
and Larry Powell.
pages cm.
Includes bibliographical references and index.
ISBN 978-1-4985-0722-6 (cloth : alk. paper) — ISBN 978-1-4985-0723-3 (electronic)
1. Political culture—United States. 2. Communication in politics—United States. 3. Political
psychology—United States. 4. Political candidates—United States. I. Powell, Larry, 1948- II. Title.
JK1726.K57 2015
111'.85—dc22
                              2015011991
ISBN 978-1-4985-0724-0 (pbk : alk. paper)

∞™ The paper used in this publication meets the minimum requirements of American
National Standard for Information Sciences Permanence of Paper for Printed Library
Materials, ANSI/NISO Z39.48-1992.

Printed in the United States of America

Contents

Acknowledgements

James T. Kitchens would first like to acknowledge his life and business partner, Elizabeth Kitchens, who encouraged him to develop and share this political model for the last eight years. He is also grateful to former U.S. Speaker of the House Jim Wright, who provided him with the opportunity to become engaged in national politics. He would also like to thank the many political consultants and hundreds of candidates he has worked with over the last twenty-five years. These experiences serve as a base of knowledge for this work. He owes a special thanks to his co-author Larry Powell for forty years of friendship and intellectual work on so many projects.

Larry Powell would like to thank his wife, Clarine Powell, for her tolerance and support while working on this project. He also wants to express his appreciation to co-author Jim Kitchens for bringing him on board for this project. Finally, he would like to thank Professor Robert Denton, of Virginia Tech, for his encouragement on this project.

Chapter One

The Four Pillars of American Politics

An Introduction

To understand why certain political messages appeal to voters, one must first understand the four pillars of the American psyche. These pillars consist of four psychological states: fear, narcissism, consumerism, and religiosity. These are the primary prisms through which Americans evaluate political messages. These four dominant components anchor the American psyche, particularly in terms of the way Americans perceive politics and government. Some may refer to this as our collective conscience. The background and development of each of these psychological states will be examined in more detail later in the next four chapters. But, for the moment, here are the four personal and societal emotional reactions associated with each one:

Fear
Attack on my home from a criminal
Attack on society by terrorists
Something could happen to my children
I could lose my job

National Narcissism
I am essential and must work all the time
My children deserve only the best
America is the greatest country
I am not responsible for anyone else
Everyone should speak English

Consumerism
I need more stuff
I should have the best

America can buy security
I am entitled to more stuff

Religiosity
There are absolute rights and wrongs
There is only one God—ours
We have some moral obligations
God loves America

These psychological states serve as attitudinal anchors, with a matrix of attitudes, beliefs, and values connecting them like a net strung between four posts. This net represents the mind. All political communications pass through this net and are evaluated based on one or more of these anchors. Then, the voter reacts to the communication. This reaction may be a positive response, a negative response, or no response. The lack of response is caused by a message being perceived as irrelevant, confusing, or simply failing to penetrate the consciousness or appealing to any of the pillars. According to Social Judgment Theory (Hovland & Sherif, 1961, 1980; Sherif, Sherif & Nebergall, 1965), there is a range of positions or latitudes which people find acceptable, unacceptable, or uncertain. For a political candidate to be considered by a voter, the candidate's message must fall within their range of acceptable ideas, or at least close to those ideas. Any message rated as unacceptable means that both the message and the candidate are dismissed by the voter. Additionally, a person's ego-involvement in an issue will determine how large the areas of acceptability and unacceptability are on any issue (Powell, 1976). The Four Pillars model differs from the traditional Social Judgment Model in that there are four specific anchors or pillars involved in the reaction to a message versus a theoretical model with no context of the American culture. Using the Four Pillars model, any number of these pillars could play a role in determining the reaction to a political message. Therefore, the most effective political message should be relevant to all four pillars.

Another factor to consider is the phenomenon known as Cognitive Dissonance, a psychological theory initially developed by Leon Festinger (1957). According to this theory, individuals become uncomfortable when confronted with or exposed to dissonant information, i.e., ideas and information that is at odds with their view of the world. When placed into a situation where they must confront dissonant information, they will engage in any of several techniques to relieve the resulting psychological discomfort. This includes rationalizing, discounting the information, or discrediting the source, among others. The idea is important in politics, since it implies that voters will be resistant to any information that might alter their views of their party or preferred candidate. In fact, voters are known to be apprehensive about even the possibility of listening to dissonant information and highly inflexible in responding to that information (Wheeless & Schrodt, 2011).

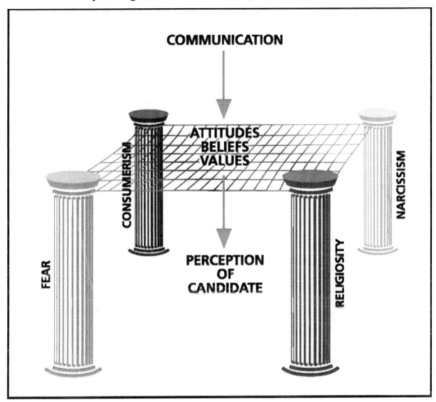

Indeed, such political attitudes are the result of a lifetime of political socialization and serve as an anchor, or political bedrock, for political preferences. As a result, party identification is more stable than any other relevant political attitude (Abramson & Ostrom, 1991; Green & Palmquist, 1994). Thus, getting a campaign message to influence someone with different political orientations is difficult—so difficult that most campaigns don't even try. Instead, they aim for the low-hanging fruit that is available from their party loyalists and try to add enough independent voters to make a majority. How successful those campaigns are often depends upon their ability to craft an effective campaign message.

Campaign messages can be analyzed using this Four Pillars model. A good political communication message should have the voters engaging several of the attitudinal anchors simultaneously. Here are two examples, one from a standard Republican message and one from a standard Democratic message.

> A Republican candidate says: *We must fight against any tax increase. It only allows the government to have more control over our freedom. It is your money and they are simply taking it from you to give it to people who won't find a job. This is wrong. We have a mission; less taxes, more freedom.*

Analyzing this statement using the model, when the voters hear this message, then all four pillars are activated. First, there is a fear appeal against a big government, i.e., a tax increase allows government to have more *control* over you. Second, there is consumerism, i.e., they are simply taking your money. This statement means you are not getting anything in return. Your money is not being used to build new roads, pay for military defense, or to keep the environment clean. Third, there is narcissism, i.e., they are giving it to people who will not work with the underlying value that you should not be responsible for them. Finally, there is religiosity with a moral judgment, i.e., this is wrong. The phrase that *this is wrong* leaves no doubt what the listener should conclude.

Here is a message the Democrats might use:

> *The Republicans have declared war on our children. Our neighborhood schools educated a generation that created more wealth and prosperity than ever before. Now, they want to take away that same opportunity from our children by stealing tax money and diverting it to private institutions who have no accountability. This idea is corrupt and immoral.*

The first statement is designed to strike the emotion of fear, i.e., your children are threatened. The second sentence hits a narcissistic chord, i.e., our generation is the best ever. The phrase that they want to take away that same opportunity actually hits at the consumerism pillar because it says they would not be able to buy the things they deserve. Finally, there are two appeals to religiosity, i.e., stealing tax money and the idea that it is corrupt and immoral. Both of these say the Republicans are taking actions that are against accepted moral behavior.

Using the Four Pillars model, it becomes clear why certain political communication styles fail to have impact on the electorate. For example, some campaigns try to use enthymemes, a form of truncated logic. This approach was originally advocated by Aristotle (Cooper, 1932, 1960), who argued that omitting one line of a logical syllogism allows the audience to complete the argument with its own premises. Thus this argument normally presents facts and allows the recipient to draw a conclusion (e.g., Conley, 1984; Paglieri & Woods, 2011; Powell, 1976).

One argument from a campaign said: *Senator Blank is going to raise the percentage of the state education budget from 55 percent to 57 percent. This will give the schools a boost without raising taxes.* Since the information is filtered through a matrix that is based on four different concepts, different voters may draw different conclusions or may miss the point and view the argument as confusing or irrelevant. This message is based upon the underlying assumption that voters think the education budget needs more money. Even given that assumption, what does this two percent mean? Are we just throwing money at a problem? Will it provide for a better education for my child? A good campaign message tells the voters both what the information means and why they should care.

Another failed strategy is to run an "egocentric biography" campaign. That is, the campaign focuses on a candidate's background and accomplishments. Such a campaign may make the candidate feel proud, but it often has little impact. While some biographical information helps establish credibility of a candidate, beyond that factor, it does not communicate any reason the voter should care. In other cases, it can actually damage the candidate—as in Mitt Romney's inability to overcome the "rich businessman" image in the 2012 presidential election (Bruni, 2012). However, every campaign feels it needs a "bio" spot to introduce the candidate (Powell & Cowart, 2013). Usually, these spots are a waste of campaign resources and have a minimum impact on voter preference.

Voters expect all candidates to reach a minimum level of qualifications for public office, a concept that political observers call "legitimacy" (Lazarsfeld & Morton, 1960). In the 2012 Republican primary, for example, Congressman Ron Paul's views on taxes (abolish the IRS) and the postal service (abolish it too) were considered so extreme that he never did attain legitimacy as a candidate with a chance to win the nomination (Saunders, 2011).

Normally, the voters do not perceive one candidate's biography as so much better than another candidate's that it becomes the primary reason for making a choice. Political communication is not a battle of resumes as if the candidates are applying for a job. Asking voters to make you a leader is more complicated than that. Voters are looking for a leader who can provide strong leadership, but also must display integrity and an empathic understanding of them the voter (Trenaman & McQuail, 1961). That last element—an empathic understanding of the voters—is a key component in the Four Pillars model. Voters want their leaders to understand them, the public.

Unless something in a candidate's biography speaks to an important psychological anchor, it is not important in the voters' final decision on whether to vote for a candidate. For example, if a candidate is attacked for being arrested for drunk driving, the voters will react through their pillar of religiosity which contains moral judgments. This message means the candidate does not hold similar morals as the voter and that information will have an impact on the voters.

The American nation's historical development as a country and its current role in the world is the foundation for the emergence of these four collective psychological states. Examining each one will help clarify their power. The next four chapters will take up that examination and look at each pillar in terms of how it was developed and how it impacts political decisions.

REFERENCES

Abramson, P. R., & Ostrom, C. W. (1991). Macropartisanship: An empirical assessment. *American Political Science Review*, 85, 181–92.

Begley, Sharon (2010, October 11). I'm mad as Hell . . . and I'm going to vote. *Newsweek*, 156(15), 28–31.

Bruni, Frank (2012, March 11). Mitt's rich predicament. *New York Times*, SR3.

Conley, T. M. (1984). The enthymeme in perspective. *Quarterly Journal of Speech*, 70, 168–87.

Cooper, L. (trans.) (1932, 1960). *The rhetoric of Aristotle*. New York: Appleton-Century-Croft.

Festinger, L. (1957). *A theory of cognitive dissonance*. Stanford, CA: Stanford University Press.

Green. D. P., & Palmquist, B. (1994). How stable is party identification? *Political Review*, 16(4), 437–66.

Hovland, C. I., & Sherif, M. (1961, 1980). *Social judgment: Assimilation and contrast effects in communication and attitude change*. Westport, CN: Greenwood.

Lazarsfeld, P. F., & Morton, R. (1960). Mass communication, popular taste and organized social action. In W. Schramm (Ed.), *Mass communication* (pp. 492–512). Urbana: University of Illinois Press.

Paglieri, F., & Woods, J. (2011). Enthymemes: From reconstruction to understanding. *Argumentation*, 25, 127–39.

Powell, L. (1976). The measurement of involvement: A comparison of two techniques. *Communication Quarterly*, 24, 27–32.

Powell, L. (1976). The enthymeme: Premises and conclusions. *The Communicator*, 6, 20–24.

Powell, L., & Cowart, J. (2013). *Political campaign communication: Inside and out*. Boston: Pearson, p. 106.

Saunders, Debra J. (2011, December 26). Extreme views keep Ron Paul from becoming serious candidate. *Birmingham News*, 11A.

Sherif, C. W., Sherif, M. S., & Nebergall, R. E. (1965). *Attitude and attitude change*. Philadelphia: W. B. Saunders.

Trenaman, J., & McQuail, D. (1961). *Television and the political image: A study of the impact of television on the 1959 general election*. London: Methuen.

Wheeless, L. R., & Schrodt, P. (2001). An examination of cognitive foundations of informational reception apprehension: Political identification, religious affiliation, and family environment. *Communication Research Reports*, 18(1), 1–10.

Chapter Two

The First Pillar of the American Psyche

Fear

Whenever fear is mentioned in America, many people recall the brave words of President Franklin Delano Roosevelt after the attack on Pearl Harbor, "We have nothing to fear, but fear itself." While the President was trying to rally the country, the truth is that twentieth-century Americans had a lot of fears from sources both real and imagined. Perhaps that is one reason that the fear is frequently used in American politics and has also been the topic of so much academic study.

Many of the early academic studies on fear appeals came from the field of social psychology. Perhaps the first was published in 1953 by Janis and Feshbach. Their study found that mild fear appeals, i.e., those that do not explicitly emphasize potential harm, were more effective than those messages which detailed specific harms that would befall those who did not follow the recommended action. Most subsequent research has supported the contention that communicators who pushed their fear appeals to too high of a level found that they ran into audience resistance to their messages. Gerald Miller (1963) subsequently provided a summary and analysis of research on fear appeals as it related to communication scholars. While the extent of the studies goes beyond the purposes of this work, the one consistent finding was that fear appeals can be highly effective as persuasive messages, if they don't go too far. Consequently, fear appeals have been frequently used in anti-smoking campaigns (e.g., Beaudoin, 2002; Thompson, Barnett, & Pearce, 2009), alcohol abuse (e.g., Weber, Dillow, & Rocca, 2011), AIDS/HIV messages (e.g., Moscato, Black, Mattson, & Blue, 2001), and a variety of other public health issues (e.g., Averbeck, Jones, & Robertson, 2011; Gagnon, Jacob, & Holmes, 2010; Hyunyi & Salmon, 2006). In addition, advertisers have continued to use fear appeals to sell a variety of commercial products (e.g., Latour, Snipes, & Bliss, 1996), including toothpaste (fear of cavities), mouth wash (fear of bad breath), deodorant (fear of offensive body odor), and air bags in automobile (fear of injury). Fear appeals have also been a major component of American religious rhetoric (e.g., Ragsdale & Durham, 1986; Jackson, 2007).

Of foremost importance to this book is the role of fear appeals in American politics. Its role is significant, leading to a situation that some authors have called "governing through insecurity" (Gagnon, Jacob, & Holmes, 2010, p. 245). The issue led one group of political researchers to ask, "Is a worried citizen a good citizen?" (Valentino et al.., 2008, p. 247). Political candidates seem to think so, because it shows up in political campaigns in negative attacks designed at scaring voters into voting against the opponent under attack (Carraro & Cartelli, 2010). The result, as Jerit (2004) noted, are campaigns beset by fear with the winner being the one who survives the attacks.

FEAR IN AMERICA

Such fear is nothing new to Americans. Outside of the academic arena, fear was a part of American life for much of the twentieth century. At the end of World War I, America emerged as a world power (Clark, 2013). We were no longer the isolated country that viewed the events of Europe as none of our concern. For a decade, America roared through the 1920s, a good economy, flapper skirts, and bathtub gin (Allen, 2010). Then, the 1929 crash of the stock market ushered in the Great Depression and our first major cause of fear in the twentieth century (McElvaine, 1993).

That fear was real for many Americans. There was a tremendous loss of jobs and the unemployment rate soared to 25 percent according to the U.S. Department of Labor. People lost their homes, their farms, and basically everything they owned. When you live in a time when a large percentage of the population are in need of the basics of life, it is understandable people were fearful. Some of the fears our grandparents felt rippled all the way down to the current generation. The "clean your plate" syndrome at meal time came out of this era when Americans feared they might not eat on a regular basis.

The fear of economics shifted dramatically on December 7, 1941, with the Japanese attack on Pearl Harbor (Gillon, 2011). Once again, Americans had a real threat that caused fear to be a part of the American psyche. The country went to war on two fronts—against a fascist madman named Hitler, who seemed to have his eyes on conquering the world, and powerful Japanese armed forces, with values of fighting to the death rather than be cap-

self-sufficiency and taking on the independence of a self-legislating body.[83]

Yet the peers' legislation will have no practical effect without the consent of the allies; so it is to winning their support that Cyrus now turns. The Hyrcanians, of course, are eager to see the Persians as strong as possible. As recent traitors and largely responsible for Cyrus's success, they fear the war will end with the Assyrians unbroken, leaving them alone to bear the brunt of their eventual wrath. Cyrus needs only remind them that their interests and his own are one and the same, because they now share a common enemy, indeed, one who hates them even more than him (4.5.23; cf. 1.5.13). The Medes prove to be the more difficult case, inasmuch as the new Persian cavalry may, in the long run, rival their own and thereby undermine their importance among the allies. Moreover, unlike the Hyrcanians, they have no fear of immediate retaliation from the Assyrians. But Cyrus plays precisely on this lack of fear to encourage their love of gain, the passion that impelled the majority of the Medes to follow him in the first place (4.2.10, 4.1.10). Accordingly, he must persuade them that the formation of a Persian cavalry promotes this end. Cyrus has been careful to lay the groundwork necessary to win the allies' acquiescence to his request. When they are out pillaging and tracking down the enemy, Cyrus orders the Persians to prepare an elaborate meal for their return and to hold off eating, because "it does not seem to me that this meal would benefit us more than appearing to care about our allies" (4.2.38). Similarly, he urges the Persians to refrain from appropriating the money left in the camp, even though they could easily do so, and instead to give it to him to distribute to the allies. His reasoning is that "it does not seem to me more of a gain to take it than to appear just to them so that they will be even better disposed to us [in the future] than they are now" (4.2.42).[84] Indeed, there could be no greater occasion for them to put their education to use than to exercise this short-term restraint for the sake of acquiring all the wealth (ὄλβον δὲ ὅλον) at a later date (4.2.46).

---

83. See Rahe 1980, for the revolutionary character of the combination of hoplite infantry with cavalry and speculations on the role Xenophon may have played in its actual introduction into Asia Minor.

84. Note the repeated stress Cyrus places on "appearance" when speaking to the peers (4.2.38 φανῆναι, 4.2.42 φαινομένους; cf. 5.3.32 πᾶσι φαινοίμεθα).

When the allies gather the next day to distribute the captured spoils, Cyrus asks them, much to their surprise, to make the division without the Persians present. He tells them that having been trusted to guard the things in the camp, the Persians will now in turn trust the allies to distribute the portions fairly. Cyrus does, however, scruple to make mention of the many horses that have been taken. The allies are, of course, free to give them to whomever they think would help them most in the field. But if they should give them to the Persians, as Cyrus now suggests, "we shall also try to do something for the common good." And where could the allies find such good and selfless friends, men who would rather prepare and serve a meal than eat it themselves, and who trust so naively in others when it comes to dividing up the spoils? The Persians appear to be those rare and much-sought-after servants who work not merely out of necessity but from goodwill and friendship too (3.1.28). Cyrus goes so far as to tell the Medes and Hyrcanians that when they rode out into danger, "we were filled with fear lest something happen to you, and mightily ashamed that we were not there with you"(4.5.48). He concludes by dismissing the suspicions of those who might fear that the addition of cavalry would make the Persians too strong. He conjures up for them the image of novice Persian horsemen falling off their mounts, one certain to cause more laughter than apprehension.[85] Cyrus's tactics are successful. The allies adopt his proposal and grant them the captured horses, although they do so in complete ignorance of the fact that the Persians are filled not with concern but with envy at the sight of them riding around outside the camp without them, that the impressive continence that Cyrus has the Persians make a show of practicing is exercised only for the sake of gaining greater pleasures later, and that their willingness to allow the allies to apportion the spoils, even to accept for the time being something less than their full deserts (4.2.43), derives not from indifference to rewards but from their desire ultimately to have it all. As for the laughter they indulge in out of confidence in their superiority in horsemanship, they forget that it might well provide a goad to push the Persians to excel, as it certainly did in the case of the young Cyrus (1.4.4–5; cf. 7.1.46).

85. Cf. 2.2.14.

Just as Cyrus convinced Cyaxares that it was in his best interest to bear the expense of arming the commoners, he now persuades the allies to provide the Persians with horses from the captured spoils. And just as in his letter to Cyaxares, the "common good" he promises to work for turns out to be much more beneficial to the Persians than to their allies.[86] This result is in perfect harmony with the hope Cyrus expresses to his own men, that the creation of a Persian cavalry will make the allies more "measured" in their dealings with them (4.3.7), the same result he thought placing a garrisoned fort among the conquered Armenians and Chaldaeans would produce among them (3.2.4). In other words, those who willingly fight on the Persians' side and those who serve out of compulsion can expect the same treatment, the only difference perhaps being that between the naked use of force and ensnarement or manipulation by guile. Deception, above all, the ability to (mis)represent the good of a part as constituting the good of the whole, is what enables Cyrus to hold together an army of disparate peoples in enemy territory. Although Cyrus does not hesitate to take very harsh measures when necessary,[87] these hardly seem to constitute the kind of "inhuman cruelty" Machiavelli maintains such a feat requires.[88] Yet there can be no doubt as to Cyrus's ultimate intentions toward the allies, and not just toward the pusillanimous Cyaxares. His plan is revealed most clearly in the message he sent back to Persia after the second battle with the Assyrian: "It seems to me that someone should go to Persia and teach them what I am saying and call upon them to send another army, at least if they wish to have the rule of Asia and possess all its fruits" (4.5.16). The empire Cyrus asks the Persians to contemplate extends not only over the conquered enemy but over their allies too, recalcitrant or not.

It would not be difficult to excuse Cyrus's treatment of the allies as the understandable, if regrettable, manipulation of foreign powers that the faithful servant of any fatherland must from time to time practice (cf. 1.6.27). This would mean that his earlier espousal of a universal brotherhood of good men was simply a piece of convenient

---

86. See 7.4.3, 7, where Adousius establishes affairs in Caria exclusively "for the good of Cyrus and the Persians," i.e., the good of their faithful allies is not considered.

87. E.g., 4.2.25, 4.4.6, 4.5.6, 7.5.31, 34.

88. Cf. Machiavelli, *Prince*, ch. 17.

political rhetoric, another instance of clothing particular interests in the garb of a more general concern. Cyrus's effort to make sure that the horses go to the Persians in particular is, strictly speaking, a violation of his professed policy of distributing rewards without regard to class or national origin (2.2.26; cf. 4.5.41 with 2.1.31 and 5.1.30). Still, it might well be that the Medes and Hyrcanians are already fully equipped with horses; and this departure from his announced principle could be easily justified on military grounds. Inasmuch as he has yet to replace Cyaxares as the effective head of the Medes, he needs a more dependable cavalry, one that cannot be withdrawn at the whim or envy of another. Nor should we forget that the universal state can only come into being through the agency of particular states or nations. Yet even after Cyaxares acquiesces to his leadership, Cyrus continues to mount Persians at a much higher rate than any others. However, before we conclude that this partisanship reveals Cyrus to be a genuine, if wily, patriot, one who surely, if surreptitiously, puts the interests of his country first, we must also note that even among the Persians, he appears to distribute the horses with an eye to something other than merit, his country's good, or even the pressing necessities of war.

The meeting at which the peers passed their law concerning horse-manship included all the captains (4.3.3). At the time, these numbered 400, and all seem to be members of the original group of peers (2.1.22). When the allies grant 2,000 mounts, all these captains become cavalry-men. Yet instead of filling their vacated places in the infantry simply with the next best men, or even with the next best Persians, Cyrus makes sure that each one appoints another peer to take his place (4.5.58). Now it is more than likely that these peers' earlier education does in fact qualify them as the next best men to become captains; and it is essential to maintain a corps of skilled officers as the backbone of the infantry. But if the peers really do excel in the infantry, why would Cyrus use any of these highly trained and specialized forces in the cavalry? Since neither commoners nor peers have experience in horsemanship, and as the peers remain much better foot soldiers, it would seem to make more military sense to keep them in their familiar positions and to train some of the more numerous commoners as cav-alry (cf. 6.1.28–29). Just as Cyrus armed only the Persian commoners for fighting at close quarters when he could have made use of at least some of the Medes as well, he now mounts the peers to the exclusion of the commoners. In the first case, we found a political subtext that he wished to keep concealed: the effective emancipation of 30,000 commoners, with all the implications this entails, was presented as a purely strategic measure. Quite apart from the present good fortune of having taken so many horses, the timing of this further transformation of the Persian army might indicate the motives behind Cyrus's procedure here. As we noted in commenting on his dealings with Cyaxares, a return to Persia is out of the question for Cyrus. But it is by no means clear that his men understand the difficulties their return would entail, or even sympathize with or care about the position in which this would place Cyrus. This is particularly true of the peers. If he originally appealed to their desire for wealth and renown, these were ultimately to be enjoyed upon their return to the city (1.5.9; 6.1.5). But inasmuch as he can now play upon these same desires to lure them into becoming cavalrymen—to transform them, figuratively speaking, into centaurs (4.3.17)—he makes it that much more difficult for them to return to their fatherland. For Persia is a poor and mountainous country, where it is difficult to ride and raise horses (1.3.3). The peers' first (and last) piece of legislation, enacted at Cyrus's suggestion, thus not only establishes their autonomy from the regime; the more successfully it is enforced, the more it renders them unfit to live in Persia again.[89] Cyrus discreetly does his best to help this process along by continuing to augment the Persian cavalry until it is both the strongest in the field—something he tells Gadatas he has "long desired"—and sufficient in number to permit *all* of the original peers and commoners to become horsemen. He does this not by following the agreed-upon principle of distributing goods on the basis of merit; rather, and by his own fiat, he makes the distribution on the basis of who first entered his service.[90] Like most of Cyrus's deeds, this, too, does not lack a colorable pretext or honorable justification: loyalty to long-standing and faithful soldiers can hardly be faulted in a general. Yet the quiet and indirect way in which he leads and manipulates even the Persians causes us to wonder whether his fellow countrymen, no less than the allies, are mere tools or instruments to his own ends (cf. 5.3.46–51).

89. Cf. 8.8.19.

90. 2.1.22, 4.5.58, 5.2.1, 5.4.32, 6.1.26, 6.2.7, 7.1.46, 7.4.12–16, 8.1.34, 8.3.16–17. For the decisive importance of cavalry, see 8.5.23.

At the beginning of the expedition, he had encouraged the peers in the hope that by putting their education more effectively to use, they could gain "much wealth, much happiness, and great honors both for themselves and for their city" (1.5.9). After the second and more profitable battle, he exhorts them to continue the fight so as "to possess ageless wealth both for us and those who belong to us" (4.2.44). Honors for themselves and for the city are no longer enumerated among the ends they are to hope for (cf. 6.1.4–5). To understand the reasons for Cyrus's modification of his earlier promise, it is necessary to examine the place of the Persians in the final disposition of his empire.

Chapter Three

Empire

Through superior preparation and tactics, Cyrus manages to defeat the numerically superior Assyrian army and its allies in one last pitched battle. The Assyrians retreat to Babylon, where they think themselves secure behind impregnable walls. Cyrus can only propose to lay siege to the city in the hope that famine will eventually compel the inhabitants to capitulate. The prospects of success seem dim. Not only do the Babylonians possess provisions enough to last them twenty years, but many of the troops Cyrus sets to guard the city are drawn from peoples who were their recent allies, and, as such, liable to be better disposed to the besieged than to the Persians. Cyrus's run of good fortune appears to have come to an end, and his army seems unlikely to hold together. But Babylon lies on the banks of the Euphrates, a great river, considered impassable by the Assyrians. Under cover of building siege works, Cyrus devises a strategy to divert its waters into ditches. On the occasion of a certain Babylonian festival, at which it was the custom to drink and revel the whole night through, Cyrus opens up the trenches and gains access to the city via the riverbed. The surprise is total, Babylon is taken and the Assyrian king dispatched (7.5.13–34).[1]

The suspicions raised at the end of the previous chapter concerning the benevolence of Cyrus's intentions toward his fellow citizens and allies seem to be allayed by his behavior following this final victory over the Assyrians and the capture of their capital.[2] After allowing the Magi to set aside the firstfruits for the gods, he proceeds to over-

---

1. On the danger of having a river run through the walls of a city, see *Hel.* 5.2.7.
2. Cf. Tatum 1989, 188–89.

see the distribution of houses and government buildings in Babylon "just as had been resolved, with the best [going] to the best," thus proving himself as good as his word and upholding the meritocracy established by his men (7.5.35; 2.3.16). Cyrus even encourages those who think themselves slighted to come forward and make their case for a different distribution. Nothing could be more equitable. Yet there is one prominent man whom he leaves unrewarded and even without a proper home: himself. This characteristic self-neglect, apparently owing to the greater pleasure he takes in giving good things to others than in keeping them for himself, helps establish Cyrus's reputation as a disinterested judge and a desirable ally (2.3.11; 4.2.37–42). It was largely on account of this reputation that the Persian commoners were willing to submit to a meritocracy in the first place, and the allies to his leadership of their coalition (2.3.15; 5.1.28). But with the Assyrian threat destroyed, the question of the source of Cyrus's generosity, always present, but somewhat obscured by the urgent necessities of war, can no longer remain submerged.

Within any meritocracy, it is always difficult for a judge to do himself justice without calling into question his motives and claim to impartiality. In Cyrus's case, the problem is particularly acute, because what he desires, and presumably deserves, is to establish himself as befits a king (7.5.37). Of course, from the point of view of Persian law, his father still remains king, both over him and over all the other Persians (8.5.22). However, the more immediate, although not unrelated, difficulty is that when it comes to assigning his own reward, Cyrus must also respect the "judgment" (γνώμη) of his friends. There is no guarantee that they are or will prove to be good and disinterested judges themselves. Indeed, part of Cyrus's concern to establish himself as befits a king derives from his desire "to appear seldom and [in a manner to provoke] as little envy (φθόνος) as possible" (7.5.37). And the envy he has most to fear is that of his closest followers (5.2.9–11; 7.5.70–71; 8.1.47; 8.5.24).[3] If Cyrus is to enjoy some institutional check or protection from such men, he must first overcome them by some other means. To this end he "contrives" the following devices.

3. Consider also the distinction between "friends" and "Persian officers" at 7.5.41, which Cyrus is careful not to make openly in their presence (cf. 7.5.45).

Contrivances

At dawn on the morning following the distribution of the spoils, Cyrus sets up court in an open place to hold audience and deal with whatever problems might be brought before him. A disorderly mob soon surrounds him and overwhelms the ability of his attendants to control it. When some friends do manage to push their way through, Cyrus reaches out to draw them near and bids them stay until the crowd has dispersed. But the crowd only grows, and not until nightfall can he be with them as promised. By then it is time to leave, and he tells them to return early the next morning in order to discuss how matters stand. The friends depart "gladly and in a rush, for they had been paying the price of [neglecting] all sorts of necessities" (7.5.37–40; cf 1.2.16). The next day, Cyrus returns to the same place, where an even greater crowd has gathered well before his friends arrive. This time, Cyrus commands the guards to admit only his friends, the officers of the Persians, and the allies. To them he complains that if great success leaves no leisure either for himself or to spend time with friends, he is willing to bid farewell to this kind of happiness. He claims that it is ridiculous for him to be cut off from those to whom he is most well-disposed and surrounded by people he hardly knows. Cyrus then makes the disarming (and false) admission that he has made a mistake:

I expected that if one of these [in the crowd] needed something from me, he would court you my friends and ask for access. Perhaps then one of you might ask, why didn't I arrange for this to be so from the beginning instead of presenting myself in the midst [of the crowd]? It was because I recognized that in war a ruler must not be late either in knowing what he must do or in doing it at the right time. And I believed that generals who are seldom seen neglect many necessary things. But now that toil-loving war has come to rest, it seems to me that my soul also deserves some rest. But since I am at a loss as to what to do so that our affairs and the affairs of others whom we must care for might be well attended, let any one who sees what is most advantageous give counsel. (7.5.45–47)[4]

Artabazus, the Mede who had fallen in love with Cyrus as a youth and who was instrumental in the deception and betrayal of Cyaxares (1.4.27–28; 4.1.22), speaks first. He willingly bore the risks and toils of

4. Cf. *Anab.* 4.3.10.

war for the sake of one day enjoying "unstinted intercourse" (ἀφθονία τῆς συνουσίας) with his beloved. But the previous day's scene has brought home to him that time spent with Cyrus is a scarce commodity. Were it possible for Cyrus to be shared out among the most deserving, this would be the thing to do; but, if not, he is willing to proclaim in Cyrus's name that all are to go away "except us, your friends from the beginning" (7.5.48–54). There is no reason to doubt that Artabazus will date the beginning of his friendship with Cyrus back to his childhood days spent in Media. Such a brazenly self-serving argument, the first open suggestion that the principle of merit should give way to that of seniority (cf. 7.4.14), provokes Cyrus and many of the others to laughter, which in turn prepares the way for a more sober assessment of the Persians' new relationship to their general.[5] Chrysantas steps forward to explain how Cyrus's policy of allowing easy and open access to himself during the war was only reasonable, because "it was then necessary to win over the multitude in every way in order that they would be willing to toil and run risks with as much pleasure as possible" (7.5.55; cf. 5.2.19). The devotion and care he lavished on the allies was based on the pressing need he had, not only of their help, but of that of other potential defectors. Only by serving his new allies well could Cyrus hope to encourage others to revolt. But the very success of their joint undertaking eliminates the Assyrian threat, destroying the basis of their mutual cooperation, and with it the motive for Cyrus's earlier self-restraint in the open or direct pursuit of his own interests. Chrysantas, the peer who often raises points too indelicate for Cyrus to make himself (8.4.11; 1.6.19), puts the matter bluntly. He reminds the peers and allies that Cyrus can now "rule not only by means [of service]" but also "has the power to acquire what is advantageous by other means." If he wants his own house, he should have it. Having uttered this thinly veiled threat, Chrysantas concludes with some gentler observations: as no place is sweeter, more pleasant, or dearer than a man's home, it would be shameful for them to enjoy their own while Cyrus lives out of doors; and if Cyrus is to be without a hearth, what pleasure would he take in ruling? No one conquers the world to get out of the cold;[6] but, having done so, there is no need for the victor to remain

5. Cf. Plato *Republic* 388c.
6. Aristotle *Politics* 1267a14.

exposed to the elements. Xenophon relates that "many" (i.e., not all) supported Chrysantas's proposal. After the vote to grant him a "home" (οἰκία), Cyrus moves into the royal palace (τὰ βασίλεια), and without further consultation or deliberation has the treasure taken from the earlier sack of Sardis conveyed there (7.5.55–57).[7]

Taken more by guile than by force, Babylon turns out to be "as hostile to [Cyrus] as a city could be to any man" (7.5.58).[8] He must therefore attend to the proper organization of his court before he can enjoy the leisure and repose he claims to seek. Reasonably enough, his first concern is for his personal safety, especially at those times when he is most vulnerable, such as when eating, drinking, bathing, or sleeping. Cyrus believes that no man can be trusted as a guard if he loves another more than his charge. He also thinks that those who have children, agreeable wives, or boyfriends are compelled by nature to love them most. Moved by such considerations, he decides to form the inner circle of his bodyguard out of eunuchs. Cyrus is not so credulous as to believe that these eunuchs will be more devoted to him than to themselves. In fact, their debased condition serves to restrict the scope of their interests or focus it entirely upon themselves. Inasmuch as "there was no man who did not think himself entitled to take advantage of a eunuch unless there were some stronger power to prevent him," they find themselves in an otherwise almost hopeless, if unnatural state. But precisely their reduction to atomized, unencumbered selves is what makes these eunuchs so useful. By honoring, enriching, and, above all, protecting his eunuchs from injustice, Cyrus manages to surround himself with guards who, if they do not prefer his safety to their own lives, at least have their own well-being and survival inextricably linked to his (7.5.59–61).[9] Given the immediate hostility Cyrus faces from his Babylonian subjects, it is no small advantage to him that the "loyalty" of these most trusted servants does not require years of education or training to inculcate (cf. 1.6.33–34; 3.1.17;

---

7. For the source of these spoils and their ultimate use, see 7.1.13, 8.4.29.

8. Cf. *Anab.* 7.7.29.

9. This interpretation of the political utility of eunuchs is compatible with and even confirmed by Xenophon's presentation of Panthea's eunuchs sacrificing themselves on her grave. According to Xenophon, suicide is by no means unreasonable under certain conditions (see 8.7.2–5; *Apol.* 1, 9; *Mem.* 1.2.16, 4.8.1–3; *CL* 10.6, 8.3, 11.4–6; *Hel.* 4.5.11–19. Cf. *Anab.* 4.7.13–14).

8.7.13–14). Yet however useful eunuchs may be, they cannot solve all of Cyrus's security problems. It is possible to redress their admitted inferiority in bodily strength with better weapons—"Iron makes the weak equal to the strong in battle"(7.5.65). But equality is not enough. The eunuchs' relatively small numbers leave them inadequate to the task, no matter how well armed, of standing up to the vast multitude of those who hate their master. Nor can Cyrus greatly increase the membership of their ranks himself, because their utility to him depends on them remaining a small, despised minority. Moreover, as their care for him depends upon their debased condition, were he at the same time the author of that condition, their gratitude for his protection would likely be diminished.[10]

Cyrus must, therefore, supplement his force of eunuchs by establishing a special corps of 10,000 Persian spearmen to guard his palace day and night and to accompany him whenever he goes out. In choosing the next-most-trustworthy guards to fill these posts, Cyrus does not look among those who served him so well during the war. Rather, he selects them from among the commoners left behind in Persia. Cyrus knows the extremes of poverty they suffer there (8.3.38). He calculates that more than any others, these men will be grateful for the kind of life he can offer them in Babylon. Indeed, the gratitude they feel at being rescued from their hard lot would seem to grow in proportion to their lack of any claim based on worth or loyal service (cf. 8.2.27). This deviation from the strict rule of merit in assigning places can no doubt be justified by the necessity of securing Cyrus's personal safety, on which now depend the safety and existence of the empire as a whole. But it is worth noting that, as with the eunuchs, Cyrus places closest to him, not those on whom he bestows some great good, but rather those whom he can protect from further and inordinate harm (7.5.66–68).

To round out these arrangements, Cyrus stations strong garrisons around the city and orders the Babylonians to pay for their support.

10. Consider the case of Gadatas, 5.3.8, 5.4.35. Cf. Herodotus 8.106. Commentators disagree whether Cyrus simply employed the eunuchs he found available in Babylon or castrated them himself, as Zonaras maintains in his paraphrase of this passage (*Epitome historiarum* 3.25). Although the Greek text is ambiguous, the sense supports the latter interpretation. Gera 1993, 203, notes that Xenophon distances himself from Cyrus's calculations on these matters.

He does not do this, strictly speaking, for the sake of defense, but, as Xenophon tells us, in order to keep his subjects destitute and therefore more submissive and easily managed. At first glance, it might seem that Cyrus is intent on establishing in Babylon the kind of political and economic conditions that contributed to maintaining the stability and integrity of the republican regime in Persia. There, a poor, numerically superior underclass balanced a small but powerful military elite. Cyrus certainly does his best to persuade the peers to continue in their practice of virtue and to educate their children in the same ancestral traditions that formed their souls. But in Persia the king had neither a bodyguard nor a special detail of spearmen to protect him and his royal palace. His position was that of *primus inter pares*, holding high religious office through a hereditary claim but bound to act in accordance with the laws and decisions of an assembly (1.3.18; 1.5.4–5; 8.5.23–24). Cyrus's institution of a bodyguard, the desire to make himself inaccessible, the extensive use of spies and cultivation of informers, the relocation of the treasury to the royal palace, and maintaining his subjects in as poor and defenseless a state as possible—all of these policies closely resemble those Herodotus tells us were established by Deioces, a man whose false reputation for justice allowed him to consummate his "love of tyranny."[11] Moreover, these measures are designed to protect him as much from his closest and ablest companions as from his unwilling Babylonian subjects (cf. 8.2.15). Indeed, the former are the true objects of his most serious concerns (8.1.47).[12]

The chief cause of Cyrus's fears arises from the nature of the kind of goods that the better sort of men pursue. Desiring something more than protection from ills or satisfactions of the body, they, like Cyrus, are moved on a deeper level by the love of honor, a love fostered in them by the Persian education and encouraged at every turn by Cyrus. Yet it is a love that must eventually set them at odds. The divisive implications of this "common" pursuit appear most clearly in an episode that takes

11. For the bodyguard, cf. 7.5.58 with Herodotus 1.98, cf. *Hiero* 6.10–14, 8.10; for inaccessibility and petitions, 7.5.57, 8.3.19 with Herodotus 1.100; for spies and informants, 8.2.12, 8.6.16 with Herodotus 1.100, for moving the treasury, 7.5.57 with Herodotus 1.98; for disarming subjects and keeping them poor, 7.5.69, 79 with Herodotus 1.98; cf. *Hiero* 5.3.
12. Cf. *Hiero* 5.1–2.

place in the midst of the campaign. Gobryas, an older man of influence under the Assyrian king, defects to Cyrus's camp shortly after the first, inconclusive battle. In this fight, the original Assyrian king is killed, and the succession falls to his son. Although Gobryas has been a most devoted friend to the father, he cannot bring himself to serve the new king, who, out of envy, had killed Gobryas's son, thus leaving him without a male heir. He now seeks to take revenge for this by helping Cyrus and declares himself willing to turn over his cavalry and fortress to the allies (4.6.2–7). Cyrus accepts this offer and leads his men to the fortress, which, after many precautions, he enters and inspects to his satisfaction. Gobryas displays the mass of wealth and provisions he has hoarded inside and turns it all over to Cyrus to make use of as he thinks fit. Only after Cyrus sees that Gobryas is true to his word, does he pledge to make good on his own promise to take vengeance on the Assyrian king. He then returns all of Gobryas's gifts, although not to him directly but to his daughter and her future husband, whoever that might prove to be (5.2.4–8).

Cyrus goes on to say that there is one gift, however, that he will not return, a gift he values more than all the wealth of Babylon, indeed, more than all the wealth of the world. Gobryas suspects that Cyrus had in mind his daughter, "a wonder of beauty and stature." Nothing could be further from Cyrus's heart (cf. 8.4.22; 8.5.28). Instead, he thanks Gobryas most of all for giving him the opportunity to show his real self, to make manifest that his true aims are above common reproach.

I think there are many human beings who would not consent to be impious or commit injustice or lie, but they die before they make clear what sort of men they are, because no one has ever seen fit to entrust them with great wealth, tyranny, fortified walls, or children worthy to be loved … but you have thus given me an opportunity of showing to all human beings that I would not do wickedness against a guest-friend or commit injustice for the sake of wealth or willingly prove false to a covenant. And so long as I seem to be a just man and am praised by human beings as such, I shall never forget nor fail to distinguish you with every honor. (5.2.9–11)

One honor, though, he immediately denies Gobryas, the honor of being trusted in return. Rather than pass the night inside Gobryas's fort, Cyrus camps outside with his troops and even refuses to eat the food offered by his host (5.2.14–15). Gobryas accepts this treatment. As a traitor to one master, he can hardly complain at being so little trusted by another; and by this time he no longer has any choice but to acquiesce (5.2.24; cf. 4.2.13). Moreover, he looks forward to payment, not in honor or reputation, but in the blood of his enemy. His highest good is someone else's harm. But there are others whom Cyrus fails to trust completely, others whom he keeps from tyrannical power and hence denies the opportunity to win the highest honor, namely, his own men. Indeed, Cyrus considers himself to be surrounded by men "who are jealous (ζηλοῦσι)[13] of me and praying to the gods that they may one day prove that they are not less faithful to their friends than I"(5.2.12). But his own love of praise stands in the way of their fulfillment. So long as they remain untested, he is not without some justification for keeping them from power; and so long as they believe the success of their common enterprise depends on Cyrus, they are more or less willing to acquiesce in his ascendency, at least in dangerous situations (3.3.10; cf. 6.1.5). Still, the desire for honor, so much encouraged by Cyrus as a goad to make them fight, must ultimately turn his men against him, especially in more peaceful times when it becomes much more apparent that the satisfaction of one presupposes the disappointment of all others.[14]

If Cyrus has good cause to distrust and fear the most capable men in his empire, he also knows that it is impossible to do without them. Were he openly to show distrust, for instance, by forbidding them to approach him or by disarming them, this would quickly lead to rebellion, civil war, and the destruction of the empire. In the face of this dilemma, Cyrus resolves to do what "he knew to be both best for his own safety and most noble: to make the best (κράτιστοι) better friends to himself than to one another" (8.1.48). Xenophon devotes an entire chapter to detailing Cyrus's techniques. First, believing it difficult for men to love someone who hates them or to hate someone who is well disposed, he always strives to display "benevolence of soul." This is nothing new. But whereas before he sought his companions' friendship by taking forethought and laboring on their behalf, now

13. For the distinction between jealousy (ζῆλος) and envy (φθόνος), see Aristotle *Rhetoric* 1388a–1388b30: "It is necessary that those who are jealous consider themselves worthy of the those goods they do not possess."

14. Cf. 8.2.27; *Mem.* 2.6.21; *Cyn.* 13.10.

that he has more money he manifests his benevolence and reminds them of his friendship by spending it on food and drink to share with them, an arrangement he finds altogether more economical (8.2.2). To increase the effectiveness of this approach, he introduces the division of labor and the principle of specialization into his kitchens in order to refine the various arts of cooking (8.2.5–6; cf. 6.2.34). And knowing that gifts that come from a king give greater delight owing simply to their origin, Cyrus takes special care to serve those he wishes to honor from the superabundance placed on his own table (8.2.3),[15] a practice that, incidentally, permits him to enjoy the benefit of having food tasters, after the manner of Astyages (1.3.9), although without an open admission of their need.[16]

As a matter of policy, Cyrus initiates the practice of giving extravagant gifts. "For although he surpassed [all] human beings in receiving the greatest income, he surpassed them still much more in giving the most gifts" (8.2.7). He seeks out the best doctors and medicines and supplies them to those he wishes to court, having observed that most human beings fail to make adequate provision for future sicknesses (8.2.24–25).[17] In the midst of this catalogue of the benefits with which Cyrus apparently provides his subjects, Xenophon mentions his establishment of an extensive network of spies and informers, the so-called Eyes and Ears of the King. The purpose of this institution is not to collect useful information, but, first and foremost, to make his subjects feel themselves under constant surveillance. Thus "no one would have dared to say anything disparaging about Cyrus to anyone else, because everyone treated whoever was present as if they were the Eyes and Ears of the King" (8.2.10–11). Mutual suspicion and distrust are the natural and intended fruits of this policy, to which Cyrus adds the mutual envy bred by open and at times arbitrary favoritism (8.2.28; 8.4.1, 5, 10–12).

What is unusual here is that Xenophon includes these divisive policies in a section explicitly devoted to showing how Cyrus made "the best better friends to himself than to one another," or, in an equally

15. Cf. *Hiero* 8.1–7.
16. Cf. Cyrus's practice with that of the more spontaneous and less successful Cyrus the Younger (*Anab.* 1.9.25).
17. Delebecque 1978, 107 n.1, identifies Cyrus as the founder of national health care and subsidized prescriptions.

ambiguous phrase, how he "hunted the friendship of his companions"
(συνόντων ... τὴν φιλίαν θηρεύειν). The "friendship" in question here
could be that between Cyrus and his companions or the friendship that
exists among the companions themselves. And "to hunt" can mean
to capture or to kill.[18] The latter possibility would seem to convey
Xenophon's intended meaning, for "to make the best better friends
to himself than to one another" requires neither the existence of any
true friendships nor precludes Cyrus's efforts to turn them against
one another.[19] This reading allows us to understand why Xenophon
includes in this chapter these and other policies intended to produce
actual harm. For instance, even the lavish gifts Cyrus bestows carry
with them a possibly unpleasant and perhaps not entirely unforeseen
consequence: by their very magnitude, they act to dissolve ties of family and kinship by making the recipients prefer Cyrus to their brothers,
fathers, and children (8.2.9; cf. 3.1.39; 5.5.28–32; 8.7.14). And if Cyrus
always appears willing to do great favors in return for small ones
(8.4.31), it nevertheless remains true that someone must pay the difference in the end (8.6.23). Cyrus's reliance on doctors to maintain the
health of his subjects also marks a change in principle from his father's
advice to concentrate his efforts on the prevention of ills, although it is
an appropriate accompaniment to the shift from a Persian to a Median diet, something he knows will result in greater intemperance and
worse health among those he feeds (1.3.4–6; 1.6.15–17; 8.1.36–37).

The final institution that Xenophon mentions in this chapter removes any lingering doubts as to the true character of Cyrus's intentions towards his men:

In addition to these things, Cyrus established it as law (ὥσπερ νόμον κα-
τεστήσατο) that whenever a judgment was called for, whether in a civil suit
or a disputed contest, those who required the judgment must concur on the
judges. Now it is clear that both antagonists would aim at having the best men
and especially their friends as judges. The loser would envy the winner and
hate those who had cast their judgments against him. The victor, on the other
hand, would pretend to have won because of the justice of his cause, holding
that he did not owe gratitude to anyone. And as in other cities, those who
wished to be first in Cyrus's friendship would also be envious of one another,

18. 1.4.5, 17; *Mem.* 2.6.29, 3.11.7–15.
19. Consider the force of δοκεῖ in the last sentence of 8.1.48; cf. 3.1.31.

so that most of them wished one another out of the way more than they did anything for their mutual good. So this makes it clear how he contrived that all of the best would love him more than one another. (8.2.27–28)

As Xenophon notes earlier, failure to show gratitude is what makes men hate one another most (1.2.7). Thus the whole procedure is well designed to stir up as much envy and ill will as possible, all the while protecting Cyrus from the responsibility for making divisive and quite possibly unpopular judgments. Notwithstanding their resemblance to legal institutions, rendering justice or establishing a common good are not among the aims of these courts.[20]

The cumulative and intended effect of Cyrus's contrivances is to drive his followers into an isolated, emasculated, and almost asocial state, not unlike that of his eunuchs. His success is such that one of the ablest officers among the Persians finally takes to swearing impotently "by Hera," the oath of a woman (8.4.12).[21] But just as Cyrus, out of a concern for his own safety, is forced to supplement his contingent of eunuchs with the 10,000 spearmen, a similar calculation limits the extent to which he can enfeeble and debase his companions.[22] Were he to push the process too far, he would stand in need of a similar supplement in order to hold the empire together. Yet there is no ready alternative. Anyone able to fill such a role would only end up posing the same threat. Cyrus must therefore mitigate the effects of his various "contrivances" against the best (κράτιστοι) by also taking care that "they remain together and not turn against their practice of virtue" (8.1.47; 7.5.70). His efforts to do so constitute a new kind of political education.

Imperial Education

Cyrus continues to employ those who helped him to victory because he judges his "mercenaries" (the eunuchs and spearmen) to be inadequate to the task of maintaining and expanding the empire by themselves. Gratitude, a sentiment made obligatory by Persian law, plays no part in his calculations. Yet what makes these men indispensable is their

20. Cf. the change from 1.3.17 and 5.1.13.
21. Cf. 1.4.12; Aristophanes *Assembly of Women* 155–56, 189–90.
22. Cf. *Hel.* 2.3.19.

practice of the kinds of virtues inculcated by those same laws. He therefore sets about as best he can to duplicate the education and institutions that fostered them. Cyrus cannot reproduce Old Persia exactly. Both the size of their new city and the wealth they now possess are incompatible with their former way of life (7.5.72; 8.3.38).[23] But an even greater obstacle to the reestablishment of Persian education proves to be Cyrus's earlier denigration of the core of that education, the practice of virtue for its own sake, and its replacement by an understanding of virtue as a means to acquire great wealth, happiness and honor. Even worse, he seems to have promised at the beginning that once victory is achieved, they will be able to abandon the onerous practice of virtue altogether (1.5.8 11; 2.1.1; 6.2.21; 7.5.80). Having discredited the traditional perspective of the republican citizen, Cyrus must find other means to achieve the results it produced. And as he does not have the same recourse either to force or long habituation, he must attempt what the enforcers of the Persian laws had dispensed with: he must present an argument to persuade his men "to realize themselves that it is best to abide in and care for virtue" (7.5.71).[24]

The argument Cyrus deploys operates on several levels. Anticipating the disappointed response of those peers who remember his first public speech in Persia—"What then is the benefit for us to have achieved what we desired if we must still endure hunger, thirst, cold, and care?"—Cyrus first and most straightforwardly tries to argue that the practice of virtue, although not good or pleasant in itself, is the necessary condition for enjoying bodily satisfactions. His claim rests on the premise that nothing can be pleasant unless it answers to some perceived need. If hunger is the best sauce, the best way to prepare it is apparently with toil (7.5.80; 1.2.8; cf. 8.2.6). The practice of virtue is also, and perhaps more clearly, necessary if they are to avoid experiencing "the harshest of all things: for not to have taken good things is not so harsh as it is painful to be deprived of them after taking them" (7.5.82). This observation would seem to counsel moderation in the acquisition of possessions that are difficult to hold on to, or, once they are acquired, to arrange for someone else to have charge of their safekeeping (cf. 8.3.42ff.). But at the moment what

23. Cf. Aristotle *Politics* 1276a26–30.
24. Cf. *Mem.* 1.2.11.

the Persians and their allies find themselves in possession of is a great empire, one whose keeping they cannot trust to others with any safety (7.5.84). Cyrus repeatedly reminds them of the dangers posed by their new subjects and of the foolishness of relying on mercenaries for their protection (7.5.73, 77, 81–84). It is, then, for the sake of enjoying bodily pleasures and to avoid being despoiled in turn that they must continue to practice virtue and impose Persian education on the children born to them in Babylon (7.5.86).

The virtue Cyrus stands most in need of in his men is "manly goodness" (ἀνδραγαθία, 7.5.82). By this he means willingness to take on every toil and risk in the conviction that it is more worthy to die in battle than to save oneself by flight, a disposition he once called "the greatest virtue of all among human beings" (3.3.51–55).[25] Yet it is by no means clear that pleasure and security are ends that can reasonably or dependably call forth or justify such self-sacrifice. Cyrus wants them to believe that the loss of empire means the loss of their individual lives. If this were strictly true, concern for their own preservation would seem to lead directly to the practice of the "manly goodness" necessary to hold it. But as the empire is maintained through a collective effort, and as its loss might not entail their deaths, especially were it to come, as is likely, at the hands of another imperial power,[26] Cyrus's argument will leave untouched and perhaps even encourage those willing to neglect or counterfeit their duty while relying on the efforts of their fellows. Xenophon has already given us a dramatic demonstration of the effect this kind of "moral reasoning" has on an army's success in war. Just before the first battle with the Medes and Persians, the Assyrian king addresses his troops in much the same manner as Cyrus now does his:

Assyrian men, now you must be good men; for now the contest is over your lives (ψυχαί), over the land in which you were born, about the houses in which you were reared, over your women and children, about all the good things that you possess. For if you conquer, you will be lords over all these things just as before. But if you are defeated, know well that you will surrender all these things to your enemy. Inasmuch as you love victory, stand and fight. For it would be foolish if one who wished to live should undertake to flee, knowing that the victors are saved, while more of those who flee are killed

25. Cf. *Symp.* 8.38; *Mem.* 4.5.6.
26. 3.1.37; 4.2.36–37; 7.2.11–12; 7.5.31–34. Cf. Thucydides 5.91.

than of those who stand fast. And it would be foolish if someone who desired money should embrace defeat. For who does not know that the victors save both themselves and what belongs to them and in addition take what belongs to the defeated, while the defeated at the same time throw themselves and everything that belongs to them away. (3.3.44–45)

After listening to this speech, the Assyrians collapse at the first attack of the Persian army, retreat into their fortifications, and then flee under cover of darkness. Moreover, the king and nearly all of the "best men" in his army are the ones who lose their lives (3.3.63–70; 4.1.8, 10). This kind of direct appeal to self-interest proves to be ineffective as a means to persuade men to practice political virtue. The so-called "free rider" problem was not unknown to the ancients (2.2.5; 2.3.3).

Although Cyrus incorporates the Assyrian's "rational" appeal to self-interest as an important part of his own exhortation to virtue, he is aware that such an argument is incomplete and by itself will likely fail. He knows that its success presupposes a prior attachment to or concern with justice on the part of his men (cf. 3.3.52–53).[27] Accordingly, he does what the Assyrian failed to do and supplements his argument with repeated assurances as to the justice of their cause. In addition, he stresses the similarities between the education he proposes and the one the peers received in Persia. But if the argument for virtue depends upon the mutual devotion to and care for fellow citizens fostered by Persian law, we have seen that this disposition is something that Cyrus also considers dangerous among his subjects and even seeks to undermine (8.1.47–48; 8.2.28). In an attempt to resolve the tension between what is good or necessary for the effective practice of virtue by his men and what is good or necessary for himself, he institutes a new understanding of justice, one that will sustain his followers' willingness to devote themselves to "manly goodness" and the other qualities necessary to maintain and expand the empire, while reducing the threat they pose to his own security and preeminence. Of course, justice can no longer be thought of as obedience to the kind of laws that both expressed and supported the way of life found in a small and isolated republican regime. Many of his followers are not peers and have therefore not been raised to feel the necessary

27. Bruell 1969, 109–11.

reverence those laws exact (1.6.33–34). Moreover, Cyrus has himself now taken the place of those laws by becoming the kind of "seeing law" whose potential for strict justice he first perceived as a child back in Persia (1.3.17).[28] This does not mean that Cyrus teaches the simple identification of justice with obedience to his will, as did his grandfather, Astyages (1.3.18). First, he no longer considers the institution of a seeing law to be superior from the point of view of justice, but now favors it instead as a means to establish good order (8.1.22). And, second, for reasons that will soon become clear, he is reluctant to leave all notions of legality behind. Indeed, he claims that the justice of his followers, in particular the justice by which they hold their many new possessions, derives from a title no less lawful than the one the peers claimed before. It even seems to rest upon a higher or more fundamental law. He tells his men: "Let no one of you believe that in having these things we possess what belongs to others. For it is an eternal law among all human beings that when a city is taken in war, both the bodies of the inhabitants and their possessions belong to those who capture it" (7.5.73). This might appear at first to be an appeal to brute force, to the principle that might makes right, or what is usually considered to be the extreme of injustice. This impression is reinforced when Cyrus immediately goes on to remind his followers that they must take special care to prevent their subjects from practicing the military arts, "because for those who are always closest to their weapons, whatever they wish for is most their own"(7.5.78–79).[29] But the open appeal to force always invites its equally (un)principled opposition by the same. And it would be particularly foolish for Cyrus to encourage such a view among those from whom he has the most to fear.

Cyrus, unlike the first Assyrian king, grounds his appeal to self-interest in his men's conviction of the justice of their cause, which in turn finds support in the divinely established order of the world. The Persians justify the empire to themselves by the claim of "being better than those they rule," a superiority made manifest to themselves and others by their success in war (7.5.78). And it is the gods themselves, Cyrus claims, who "have revealed [military science and discipline] to be

28. Cf. Aristotle *Politics* 1269a8–12, 1286a9–16.
29. Cf. *Anab.* 3.1.26–30.

the instruments of freedom and human happiness for human beings"
(7.5.79). They would therefore seem to sanction the predominance of
those who master them (7.5.79; cf. 1.6.5–6). Thus Cyrus insists that
the Persians and their allies owe "the greatest gratitude to the gods
because they have granted us what we believed we deserved"(7.5.72).
Surely they would not reward those who fall short in merit. To believe
then in the justice of the law of conquest, as Cyrus encourages his
followers to do, means to believe somehow in the justice and efficacy
of divine providence. Yet it is by no means clear that giving men their
due suffices to earn their gratitude. As we have seen, especially but not
only in his arrangements for adjudicating disputes, Cyrus is careful not
to count on the gratitude of those who receive only what they take to
be their just deserts (8.2.26; cf. 1.6.11; 3.1.29–30; 8.7.13). Moreover,
too great a trust in providence can lead to complacency, rash acts,
and, ultimately, failure (1.6.6). Cyrus must accordingly make some
qualifications in his teaching.

Having just evoked their success as tangible proof of their justice,
Cyrus now admits that to win an empire "*often* falls to those who have
shown only boldness." However, to win and then preserve an empire,
something that requires moderation, continence, and unflagging care,
this would provide conclusive evidence of their worth and hence of the
justice of their cause (7.5.76). But this means that their sure conviction
of the latter depends upon their continued success, while that success
in turn depends upon the justice of their cause. The argument proves
to be circular. To escape this complication, Cyrus must again have
recourse to the gods. Yet now he tells his men that the support of the
gods depends less on the Persians' own (as yet unproven) worth than
it does on the wickedness and transgressions of their enemies. "We
must consider the gods to be with us, for we have not unjustly come
into empire by plotting against others (ἐπιβουλεύειν), but, plotted
against, we took vengeance." This, and not the conviction of their own
superiority or merit, is what Cyrus finally claims is most important for
them to believe (7.5.81–82).[30]

The belief that the gods will be with them not because they are
good but because their enemies are bad is in keeping with the generally negative orientation of political relations in Cyrus's empire. The

30. Cf. *Anab.* 3.1.21–22.

advantages of this teaching for Cyrus are several. First, as the risks
and sacrifices necessary to take vengeance are similar to those necessary to maintain and expand the empire, the Persians' belief that they
are divine instruments will make them more willing to face the necessary dangers in the hope or expectation that the gods will be protecting
them (1.5.14). And by emphasizing the wickedness of their opponents,
Cyrus again brings home to them the pressing need they have for such
protection, to say nothing of their own vigilance. Second, the anger and
indignation that necessarily accompany calls for vengeance encourage
a kind of self-forgetting that similarly leads them to put their own lives
and interests at risk.[31] Third, this focus directs his men's attention away
from their own qualities as the basis of their claim to rule and therefore
mutes the potential for rivalry and competition that such claims might
raise against their own ruler, whom they gradually come to regard as
the favorite of the gods.

Fourth, and perhaps most important, Cyrus's teaching injects into
the empire something of the moral psychology characteristic of the
republican dedication to law. As Cyrus explains, the mere fact that he
and his men now possess the majority of good things will cause almost
everyone else to envy them, to plot against them, and to become their
enemies. The Persians, we recall, believe that they were justified in
seizing the empire on account of the Assyrians' having initially plotted
against them (1.5.13); and now the possession of that empire virtually
guarantees the continued existence of others who will stand in need of
similar chastisement. Almost everyone, it seems, must be assumed to
be plotting against them. If such a disposition merits punishment, and,
moreover, a punishment apparently sanctioned by the gods, then the
Persians must regard their enemies not merely as opponents but as
transgressors, who could have held themselves back if only they had
made sufficient effort (cf. 5.1.11, 14). In other words, Cyrus encourages
his men to hold everyone, even their enemies, to the same strict
standard imposed by the Persian republic on its own citizens: the mere
desire or inclination to wickedness is considered culpable (1.2.3).[32]

---

31. Cf. *Anab*. 5.3.3.
32. The attitude Cyrus inculcates in his men recalls that of the Spartans toward
the Plateans (Thucydides 3.68). Orwin 1994, 77–78.

This argument is unlikely to persuade the Persians' neighbors to acquiesce in their subordination. And Cyrus, unlike the Persian laws, makes no pretense that such a policy is in the service of the common good (cf. 1.2.2). His words are intended for internal consumption and to hold his own men in check. This audience is of particular importance to Cyrus. For with the establishment of the empire, it becomes clear that, among the victors, it is he who possesses most of the good things and occupies the highest place. According to the logic of his own argument, which he elsewhere admits, as king he must of necessity be plotted against (8.7.12). Insofar as he can persuade his followers to believe that their rule rests on the gods' desire to see the wicked punished, he encourages them to consider their own inclinations to envy and plot against him as equally culpable and therefore subject to the same wrath. In Cyrus's empire, fear of divine punishment and the sentiment of religious awe assume a political importance unknown in the republic (8.1.25; 8.3.11–15). Yet this piety, however useful, rests or depends upon a prior and deeper concern with what is "fitting." Above all, Cyrus insists that his men must believe that it is not "fitting for one who is himself wicked to punish others on account of their own wickedness."[33] In this way, the argument Cyrus gives to justify the empire imposes on his subjects the duty to struggle against their own inevitable desires to envy and plot against him (7.5.84; cf. 3.1.12). Whereas the republican education of Old Persia sought to promote the common good by aiming to make its citizens such as not even to desire to commit any wicked deed (1.2.3), the modified education Cyrus gives his subjects aims to make them such as not even to desire to commit any wickedness against him.

If what is "fitting" obligates his subjects to refrain from the crimes they claim to punish, this does not exhaust its demands. According to Cyrus: "In addition, we must know well that there is no such guard as that one be himself noble and good. This [conviction] must accompany [us]. For it is not fitting that anything else be noble for one who is bereft of virtue" (7.5.85). It proves to be as difficult to divorce his men's concern with their virtue and the justice of their rule from the concern

---

33. Cyrus invokes "the fitting" (προσήκει) three times in just six or seven lines of text at 7.5.83–84. This is immediately followed by Chrysantas's related appeal to what is "seemly" (καθήκη) at 8.1.4. Cf. 2.1.15, 17; 2.3.8; 5.1.16; *Anab.* 3.2.16–17.

with their own goodness and nobility, as it is to induce them to practice political virtue simply by an appeal to pleasure or self-interest.[34] Yet the account Cyrus gives of their justice and nobility remains problematic. At the beginning of the war, Cyrus rallied and inspired the peers by an appeal to a common understanding of justice, the right of self-defense against an unprovoked enemy attack (1.5.13). The new understanding of justice that he insinuates into his followers' education—the right to punish those who plot against them—represents not so much a departure from as a radical expansion of the generally accepted principle of self-defense: to punish those who plot (or as is almost always the case with plotting, to punish those whom you suspect of plotting) is to punish those who might possibly do you harm, which means simply to take forethought for your preservation. Yet such an expansion of the just claim of self-defense removes all sense of the restraints and limitations usually imposed on us by justice, save for the prudent calculation as to whether one can act preemptively without harming oneself in the process (cf. 3.1.15; 1.6.26).[35] Moreover, this new understanding of justice actually undermines the peers' original claim to be fighting in a just cause, because it can equally serve to justify or exculpate the Assyrians' original decision to attack. According to the principles Cyrus sets down here, the Assyrians, by virtue of being at that time the larger, more successful power, must naturally have considered themselves to be envied and therefore plotted against by the Medes and Persians. In fact, with Cyrus's encouragement, the peers did come to covet the Assyrians' possessions, and well before the beginning of actual hostilities (1.5.9; cf. τὸ δόξαι at 1.5.13). The attack by the "aggressor" is, then, no less just than the defense put up by the "innocent." True, Xenophon tells us that the Assyrians sought to invade not out of fear and a far-sighted regard for their self-preservation against these others' imperial ambitions, but rather because their king "believed that if he should reduce the Medes he would easily come to rule over all those around" (1.5.2). However, this observation only highlights the difficulty of distinguishing between just and unjust aggression once Cyrus's perspective has been adopted, and increases the suspicion that his ascription of wickedness to the empire's enemies

34. Cf. *Mem.* 4.2.11–40; 4.6.5–6.
35. Cf. Plato *Republic* 351a–d.

merely serves as cover for his own perhaps equally unprincipled desire "to rule over all those around" (7.5.77 with 1.5.3; 1.6.8). Or perhaps we are to consider the ultimate subjugation of "the Indian," who once sent aid, as justified by some later transgression that outweighs the gratitude Cyrus would otherwise seem to owe him for services rendered at a particularly delicate moment (1.1.4; 8.6.20; 3.2.28; 6.2.1–11).

Cyrus's account of the nobility of his followers suffers from the opposite defect of his account of their justice. Whereas he expands the claims of self-defense to the point where they overwhelm all other considerations for restraint, he narrows his men's conception of nobility to the point where he deprives it of any intrinsic dignity or worth. The tension between the noble and the good, present whenever (political) virtue is practiced for its own sake, and without which nobility seems to lose its particular attractions,[36] dissipates as the inevitable consequence of Cyrus's earlier teaching that virtue is simply a means to other goods (1.5.8–10). But this process takes some time to run its course. In the immediate aftermath of his "corruption" of the peers' original view, Cyrus can still move them by an appeal to the noble with almost no regard for its consequences: "What ... is more noble than aiding friends?" (1.5.13). But by the end of the war, and with the addition to their ranks of commoners and others who lack the peers' original education, he is compelled to present being "noble and good" (καλός κἀγαθός) as for the most part just another "guard" (φυλακή) or means to ensure their safety within the empire (7.5.84). Cyrus seems to be aware that an education that explicitly teaches the instrumental practice of virtue and nobility will lack the substance to call forth the positive devotion that his empire still requires. He is, therefore, careful to leave his followers with at least one virtue that they can still seem or believe themselves to practice for its own sake. Because the eternal and universal law of conquest gives them the right to the bodies and possessions of their subjects, Cyrus claims, "it will not be by injustice then that you keep what you have, but it will be by benevolence (φιλανθρωπία) that you refrain from taking something away if you allow them to have anything" (7.5.73). Cyrus may always practice benevolence with other ends in sight (8.2.1–2; 1.4.1; 4.2.10), but here he encourages his men to do so for its own sake, independent

36. Pangle 1994, 139–40.

of any further calculation or considerations. Yet the anemic and truncated character of this benevolence, consisting as it does in holding
back from complete or further depredation rather than in rendering
positive benefits, remains a hollow substitute for the peers' original
understanding of justice as devotion to the common good.

According to Cyrus, a single speech or argument (λόγος) by itself
cannot lead human beings to the practice of virtue (3.3.51ff.). He
therefore supplements his own with several of the techniques employed under the Persian republic to habituate its citizens to virtue,
although with important modifications. For example, in Persia, they
sought to inculcate continence and moderation and develop military
skills by taking the young on hunting expeditions, by having them camp
out each night to guard the public buildings, and, above all, by putting
constantly before them the sight of their elders practicing these virtues.
Cyrus, too, takes care to encourage these virtues by leading his men on
hunts (although apparently not as often as in Persia),[37] by displaying
himself as the embodiment of their conscientious practice, and by
watching to see that others do the same (8.1.30–31, 35–36; 7.5.85).
Obedience to the elected officials in Persia finds its counterpart under
the empire in obedience to Cyrus. And whereas the peers in Persia
held themselves ready to carry out the commands and requirements
of the Council of Elders (1.2.5), they now agree, at the prompting
of Chrysantas, "always to report at the gates [of the palace] and offer themselves to Cyrus to use in whatever way he wished" (8.1.5; cf.
1.3.18). Chrysantas senses some reluctance on the part of the peers to
adopt this last measure, and assures them that they will differ from
slaves in serving not by compulsion but voluntarily. They can submit to
this because Cyrus, unlike a master with his slaves or a keeper with
his herds (1.1.2), will not use them for his own good and at their expense, "because the same things are advantageous for [both] of us, and
our enemies are the same" (8.1.5; cf. 1.5.13). Still, once they pass this
resolution,[38] Xenophon no longer refers to them as "peers" (ὁμότιμοι,

37. Among the "necessities" keeping Cyrus from the hunt, perhaps not the least is
that of being accompanied by his circle of eunuchs (8.1.38; cf. 8.3.19).

38. Gera 1993 282, complains that with the exception of Cyaxares' speech at
4.1.13–23, "there is never any opposition to [Cyrus's] proposals," a fault she ascribes
to Xenophon's tiresome didacticism and overriding desire to idealize his hero. Yet both
here, and as earlier noted at 7.5.57, two of the more momentous decisions sealing the

"alike or equals in honor") but as "nobles" (ἔντιμοι). This term is first introduced to designate certain subjects of the Armenian king, a man who is himself admittedly a kind of slave (3.1.8, 11).[39]

Cyrus may plausibly present himself as a model (παράδειγμα) to be imitated in the practice of continence, moderation, military prowess, and at least a certain kind of limited justice (8.1.12, 21, 27, 30–31); he cannot, as could his father, do the same with regard to obedience. If his men count on the alleged harmony of their interests with those of Cyrus to ensure that their pledge of strict obedience will not be abused, Cyrus trusts to other means to obtain their continued deference. For example, should someone think to show "greater independence" (ἐλευθερώτερος) not by refusing to obey a summons but simply by failing to do so "quickly," Cyrus isolates and dishonors him without any further inquiry (8.3.21; cf. 3.1.10–11). And those who obey "without excuses" are honored even more highly than "those seeming to offer the greatest and most toilsome virtues" (8.1.29). By allowing that this neglect was of those "seeming" to practice virtue, Xenophon spares Cyrus the outright charge that he prefers to reward the subservient rather than the good. Yet, contrary to what Chrysantas has promised, Cyrus frequently arranges matters with an eye simply to what is best for him (e.g., 8.1.9, 12; 8.3.6–13, 21; 8.4.5, 11) and honors most of all those who gratify or please him, regardless of their merits (e.g., 8.2.3; 8.3.5, 13; 8.4.1). The increasingly visible divergence between his own interests and those of his followers accounts in large measure for Cyrus's concern "to display himself toiling more and more over the things of the gods" and to promote a similar piety in his men. Xenophon tells us that "Cyrus believed that the piety of those with him was also good for himself, calculating just as do those who choose

---

fate of the peers, Xenophon indicates the presence of an opposition in a manner that reflects its precarious situation. Contrast πολλοί at 8.1.6 and 7.5.57 with πάντες at 4.2.47, 4.3.23, 5.1.29, and 6.1.19–20.

39. Carlier 1973, 152 n. 49, "L'argument [de Chrysantas] est habile, mais le critère d'obéissance volontaire ne permet pas d'établir une distinction nette entre hommes libres et esclaves.... La suite du texte affaiblit considèrablement cette opposition.... Le seul critère qui dans la *Cyropédie* fonde la distinction entre hommes libres et esclaves, c'est la différence d'activité. Si l'on adopte le critère grec traditionel de participation politique, il est bien évident que dans l'Empire perse, tous sont les esclaves sauf un.'" Pangle 1994, 149: "Even at its best, the new Persian virtue substitutes courtiership for citizenship."

to sail with the pious rather than with those who seem to have been impious in something. In addition to this, he calculated that if all his partners were pious, they would be less willing to do anything impious both concerning each other and concerning himself, for he believed he was a benefactor of his partners" (8.1.25).[40] Yet fear of the divine does not act with the same efficacy in each and every case (3.3.58). The results of Cyrus's efforts illustrate this point. If the Persians "at first" imitate him in the belief that they will become happier by serving the gods, they ultimately come to do so more for the sake of pleasing him (8.1.24; cf. 8.8.4).

Cyrus is aware of the power that his watchful gaze has on the comportment of his subjects and seeks to increase its power and range by various means. Under the republic, the peers possessed a certain security in their property rights (1.3.17). But in the empire, Cyrus comes to own everything, at least in principle (8.1.22). He uses this power to compel the nobles to attend him at court, where he can keep an eye on them. For example, anyone with sufficient means who fails to present himself is immediately considered absent owing to some incontinence, injustice, or neglect of duty, and investigated accordingly (8.1.16). Attendance is further encouraged by Cyrus's "giving the easiest and most profitable assignments" to those who are present (8.1.19). And if these measures fail to have their intended effect on a recalcitrant subject, Cyrus takes away "all that he has and gives it to another whom he thought would present himself when wanted" (8.1.20). Xenophon indicates the general effect of this policy when he reports that "[Cyrus] therefore produced *at his gates* much good order among the worse, who deferred to their betters, and much respect and decorous behavior toward one another. You would not perceive anyone *there* shouting in anger or taking pleasure in hubristic laughter, but on seeing them you would think that in reality they lived nobly" (8.1.33; emphasis added).[41] How these men behave elsewhere

40. Cf. Aristotle *Politics* 1314b39–1515a3: "Further, [the tyrant] must always show himself to be seriously attentive to the things of the gods. For [men] are less afraid of being treated contrary to the laws in some respect by such persons, if they consider the ruler a god-fearing sort who takes thought for the gods, and they are less ready to plot against him as one who has the gods as allies. In showing himself this way, however, he must avoid foolishness."

41. Cf. 8.1.39; *Anab.* 1.9.15.

when out of his sight, Cyrus can only imagine. Even with the extensive use of spies and informants, he cannot reproduce the level of mutual surveillance found in the small, austere republic.[42] We, as readers, see and hear in Babylon what was absent, or at least out of sight, in Persia: the establishment of wealthy private households and the expression of dissent (8.3.35–48; 8.4.31).[43] The political virtue of Cyrus's subjects necessarily suffers.

As the best of rulers, Cyrus cannot exercise his own virtues to their fullest extent without undermining those of his subjects. In this he resembles Aristotle's "king over all," whose excellence overwhelms any political way of life,[44] or Machiavelli's "virtuous tyrant," whose pursuit and exercise of freedom deprive all others of theirs.[45] True, Cyrus sends out satraps to govern the distant conquered nations and exhorts these men to imitate him in everything they do (8.6.9–12). But to prevent them from "immediately becoming his rivals," he makes sure that the garrisons in their cities remain under a separate command and sends out inspectors from time to time in order to lend help or "moderate" those who stand in need of it (8.6.1–4, 16).[46] These governors therefore lack the independence from any higher authority that is characteristic of Cyrus's own rule.

Cyrus apparently does not consider his claim to rule on the basis of his excellence to be incompatible with the use of cosmetics and other spells "to bewitch" his subjects. For example, he and his men begin to wear makeup so that their complexions will appear "better than they were by nature," and Median robes that hide bodily defects and make their wearers appear "especially tall and beautiful" (8.1.40). Cyrus even goes so far as to put lifts in his shoes and to make the driver of his chariot appear short, "either in reality or by some other means," so that he himself seems "much taller."[47] The larger purpose of these and other similar measures becomes clear

---

42. 1.2.7, 12, 14; *CL* 4.4–5.

43. Gera 1993, 296.

44. Aristotle *Politics* 1285b29–30; 1284b25–34. Carlier 1973, 157.

45. Machiavelli, *Discourses*, 2.2. In elaborating the concept of a "virtuous tyrant," Machiavelli makes explicit reference to Xenophon, although to the *Hiero*, not the *Cyropaedia*. From a certain perspective, Hiero and the Cyrus of book 8 are indistinguishable.

46. For the means used to induce this kind of moderation, see 3.1.27; 3.2.4.

47. Cf. *Mem.* 2.1.22; *Oec.* 10.2–7.

when he rides out for the first time in a magnificent and carefully or-
chestrated procession: "On seeing [Cyrus], all prostrated themselves
(προσεκύνησαν), whether because some had been ordered to begin it or because they were struck by the preparation and by Cyrus
seeming to appear tall and beautiful. Previously, no Persian used to
prostrate himself before Cyrus" (8.3.14).[48] The full import of this act
and the resonance it would have had for Xenophon's contemporaries
can be better appreciated in light of a passage from the *Anabasis*.
There, Xenophon reminds his fellow Greeks, "To no human being as
a despot but to the gods alone do you prostrate yourselves."[49] The
most impressive adornment with which Cyrus beautifies his rule and
bewitches his subjects is the aura of divinity that seems to attach itself
to him. At first, this is simply by virtue of his success, but later he
takes some care to cultivate it; his non-Persian subjects seem particularly inclined to regard him as the offspring of some god (4.1.27;
7.2.24; cf. 1.2.1).

The claim to rule based on excellence can go hand in hand with
the use of these and other cosmetic props that serve as signs of or
substitutes for virtues that the less discerning are perhaps unable to
detect or judge. Nor does anything prevent the most excellent from
also being the most beautiful or the favorite of the gods. But there
is no guarantee that these different and potentially rival principles
will always coincide, as they now appear to do, in one and the same
person.[50] Yet by allowing the legitimacy of his regime to rest in part on
his descent from the gods (at least within the minds of many, if not all, of
his subjects), Cyrus introduces an essentially hereditary principle that
by his own admission often stands in opposition to that of merit (1.6.8;
2.2.26). At first this claim manifests itself in the special insignia that
only Cyrus's relatives are allowed to wear and in the special property
rights enjoyed by the descendants of his original friends (8.3.13; 8.6.5).

48. Non-Persians have prostrated themselves to Cyrus before this: a group of
captured prisoners at 4.4.13, and, equally telling, the eunuch Gadatas at 5.3.18. Cf.
7.5.32. Too 1998, 298, overlooks the earlier passage when she asserts: "It is no accident
that until the final book of the *Cyropaedia* the only person to bow down to Cyrus
was the Assyrian eunuch Gadatas."
49. *Anab.* 3.2.13; cf. *Hel.* 4.4.6.
50. Cf. 1.2.1; 1.3.3; 1.4.3; *Oec.* 6.15–16.

But its most important consequence is to limit Cyrus in his choice of a successor.[51]

Given the importance of a male heir once the hereditary principle is introduced, Cyrus is fortunate enough to have two legitimate sons. Should something happen to one of them, he would not find himself in the same desperate position of a Gobryas or a Croesus (4.6.2; 7.2.20). As it is, both sons survive to maturity and are alive at the time of their father's death. We would expect Cyrus to have taken special care for their education, much as his own father apparently did for him (1.6.2–8), or even more so. In the empire, the king acts according to his will or judgment, not the law (8.1.22; 8.8.1). Here, more than elsewhere, good administration depends upon his good character (8.1.8).[52] Yet the only evidence Xenophon provides us of Cyrus taking any care for his children's education is a single speech (λόγος) of three or four minutes' length,[53] delivered from his deathbed in Persia, where he has been visiting, at a time when his sons just "happened" to be accompanying him (8.7.5).[54] If two sons are better than one from the point of view of ensuring a legitimate heir at the time of his death, their existence poses certain difficulties when it comes to choosing one as monarch. The primary aim of the speech is not their education but to make clear to them the succession of the kingship. Cyrus settles upon the eldest, Cambyses, and gives two reasons for his choice. First, since he is older "it is likely" (εἰκός) that he has more experience. But as this

---

51. See 8.7.11, θεῶν τε διδόντων καὶ ἐμοῦ.

52. *Poroi* 1.1.

53. Gera 1993, 125, claims that Cyrus's words "here anticipate (and virtually refute in advance) a criticism of the Persian king found in a chronologically later composition, Plato's *Laws*. The Athenian stranger of the *Laws* claims that Cyrus had left the education of his sons to women and eunuchs and suggests that this is why Cambyses was such a notorious failure. In our chapter of the *Cyropaedia* [8.7] Xenophon demonstrates that Cyrus *did* devote time and energy to the moral instruction of his sons and consequently should not be held responsible for subsequent events." Whether or not we hold Cyrus ultimately responsible for subsequent events (cf. 3.1.38), if we judge the "time and energy" he devotes to his children's education in the light of his own explicit standards, we are compelled to conclude that it fell well short of what he thought required for "moral instruction" (cf. 3.3.51–55; 1.6.34). Cyrus's implicit judgment of his death-bed exhortation is entirely compatible with the conclusion of Plato's Athenian Stranger (8.7.24, "Εἰ μὲν οὖν ... εἰ δὲ μή ...").

54. "Happened" translates ἔτυχον, which often has a connotation of "chance," although the presence of his sons is perhaps more than fortuitous here. See 7.2.2 with Tatum 1989, 151.

is only a likely argument, Cyrus backs up his decision with an appeal to tradition. He was himself educated in Persia to defer to his elders, not just to older brothers but to all older citizens. So they should now accept his judgment "on the grounds that what I am saying is ancient, habitual, and lawful" (8.7.10; cf. 6.1.6).

Cyrus fully expects his younger son, Tanaoxares, to be disappointed and offers him the satrapies of Media, Armenia, and Cadusia in consolation, reminding him of the endless troubles that accompany kingship and arguing that his smaller inheritance is in fact the preferable one. Without the burdens of being king, he will enjoy "a happiness free from pain, for I do not see what sort of human delight you will be lacking: all the things that seem to delight human beings will be at hand for you" (8.7.12). Of course, the range of delights available to a "human being" might turn out to be limited in certain respects. Tanaoxares' subordinate status, even as the governor of several satrapies, cuts him off from enjoying the pleasures and privileges of a "real man" (ἀνήρ). It is a position Cyrus would never acquiesce to for himself (cf. 7.2.28; 3.1.11; 1.1.1).[55] Moreover, as the weaker party, Tanaoxares must ultimately find himself at the mercy of his older brother's inclinations (cf. 1.6.10).

Cyrus can make these arguments against the desirability of being king in the presence of his elder son precisely because he considers them defective. It is literally impossible for him to imagine that anyone would actually be swayed by them to turn down the office. But he does anticipate that Cambyses might also find the terms of the bequest less than perfect. The stress Cyrus places on the need this future king will have of "trustworthy friends" to support his rule and the likelihood of finding such a one in his brother, belies the reasonable fear that Cambyses will regard Tanaoxares as his most dangerous rival, especially as he will control three contiguous satrapies (cf. 8.6.1). Cyrus exhorts Cambyses to consider their consanguinity and common upbringing in close familiarity as a foundation to be built upon with other friendly deeds. The advice he offers echoes and improves upon that given in the *Hiero* by Simonides,[56] who claims that the good ruler should consider

---

55. Gera 1993, 106.
56. Carlier 1978, 156 n.56. For similarities between Simonides' suggestions and Cyrus's actual institutions, see *Hiero* 9.1–6 with *Cyro.* 8.2.26–27; *Hiero* 11.13 with

(νομίζειν) his fatherland as his estate, its citizens as comrades, his friends as children, and his sons as his own soul. Cyrus goes one step further in telling Cambyses to regard his brother as himself (8.7.15; *Hiero* 11.14). Although such beliefs might encourage a ruler to act somewhat more benevolently, in truth one's sons are not one's soul, and neither is a brother the same as oneself.[57] Indeed, there is nothing in the argument that would induce Cambyses to prefer Tanaoxares to a trusted and less threatening servant (such as Chrysantas was for Cyrus), while there are powerful considerations that counsel against relying on him.[58] When rule passes along hereditary lines, consanguinity drives ambitious men apart, a fact that no doubt explains much of Cyrus's apparent reluctance to educate his sons in the skills and discipline necessary to rule. He therefore turns to other means to assure their cooperation. Cyrus invokes the fear of his immortal soul and the vengeance it will take on them should they quarrel. But if they doubt that the soul continues to exist after death, a doubt Cyrus himself would seem to have felt (8.7.27; cf. 7.3.14), "then out of fear of the everlasting gods who are all-seeing and all-powerful and hold the order of the whole together, unimpaired, without age or defect, indescribable in beauty and greatness, never either do or purpose anything unholy or impious" (8.7.22). Were this not enough to convince them to behave, Cyrus also points out that unjust deeds, especially when committed against those who are most closely related in friendship or family, ultimately become manifest to all, destroying the basis of trust among human beings and with it the possibility of safe, stable rule (8.7.23).

It might seem odd that Cyrus admits the possible inadequacy of the arguments he has thus far presented. But he can apparently do this because he has saved what he claims to be his strongest point for last:

Now if what I am teaching (διδάσκω) is sufficient to make you be toward one another as you ought, [then fine]; but if not, learn from what has happened in the past, for that is the best instruction (ἀρίστη διδασκαλία). Many parents have gone through their lives as friends to their children, and many brothers with their brothers. But some of these have acted in a contrary way. Whichever

---

Cyro. 8.2.16ff.; *Hiero* 11.10 with *Cyro.* 8.6.23; *Hiero* 8.4 with *Cyro.* 8.2.8, 25; *Hiero* 8.3 with *Cyro.* 8.2.28; *Hiero* 11.3 with *Cyro.* 8.6.11; *Hiero* 11.4 with *Cyro.* 8.6.16; *Hiero* 11.7 with *Cyro.* 8.7.8.

57. Strauss 1968, 142 n. 10.
58. Cf. *Hel.* 6.4.33; Herodotus 3.30ff.

of these ways you might perceive to have been advantageous, you would deliberate correctly in choosing it. (8.7.24; cf. 1.6.45)

Cyrus's admonition to learn from the past recalls Xenophon's own willingness to look for guidance in political life through the study of "the things that have happened," that is, from history in its premodern sense (1.1.3). But if the events surrounding the transformation of the son of an obscure king in a small and remote country into the absolute monarch of virtually all the known world could capture the interest and imagination of a writer from a distant time and place, how much more influence must Cyrus's example exercise over the hearts and minds of his children. Herein lies the problem. Cyrus may call upon "the ancient, habitual, and ancestral" to justify his decisions and to guide the behavior and thoughts of others; he may even claim to have deferred at all times to his older brothers and older citizens; but the deeds that led to his success show him to have operated on somewhat different principles. We need only recall that his first public address contained a thoroughgoing attack on his elders for adhering to the traditional Persian practice of virtue; that he deceived, manipulated, and ultimately deposed his older uncle from the command of his own and the allied troops; and that his conscious and deliberate transformation of the defensive action against the Assyrians into a war of imperial conquest stood in defiance of his father's counsels and quite possibly his explicit commands (1.6.6, 26–46; 6.1.4). As for the treatment that an actual brother could have expected at his hands, there is no reason to think it would differ in essentials from that which his uncle Cyaxares received. Moreover, the example of Cyrus's considerable success as an only child would likely serve to remind his sons how well each could do without the other. Gera claims that Cyrus's "very last words to his sons are a clarion call for love and loyalty between brothers."[59] What he actually says is this: "Remember this last thing from me, that by benefiting your friends, you will be able to punish your enemies" (8.7.28). Had Cyrus made manifest the solid foundation or intrinsic goodness of such friendship and demonstrated that brothers necessarily partake in it, perhaps his parting words could be made to bear the interpretation Gera gives them. But given the absence of

59. Gera 1993, 124.

such an argument and taken as they stand within the context of his final speech—indeed, within the context of his life as a whole—they read more as an incitement to fraternal strife than concord.

Collapse

In order to maintain the empire, Cyrus seeks to bind his subjects to himself and one another through a shared self-understanding of themselves as instruments of a divinely sanctioned vengeance against their foes. But to secure his own position within that empire, he is forced at the same time to undermine the mutual devotion to one another that serves to make them useful and dependable subjects. The policy of continual expansion, which follows from the new understanding of virtue and justice he propagates, helps Cyrus to maintain a delicate balance between these contrary forces, first by keeping his treasury full, and second by ensuring the constant presence of a common enemy. Yet the synthesis or amalgam of Persian "firmness" (καρτερία) with Median "splendor" (ἁβρότης), held together in the person of Cyrus only through a supreme effort of will and at considerable human cost (5.1.5–8), proves unstable when extended to a wider circle. Over time, it issues in a general decline into "Median softness" (8.8.15).[60] After Cyrus's death his sons "immediately" fall into dissension, and the empire "immediately" splits along its deep internal fissures and descends into civil war.[61] The emphasis Xenophon places on the speed and irreversibility of this collapse makes it unlikely that he simply intends to convey the proverbial message that all regimes are ultimately doomed to decay and gradually pass away.[62]

Xenophon devotes the final chapter of the *Cyropaedia* to a detailed examination of the character of the Persians' moral and military degeneration. In the first 2,100 years or so following the appearance and wide circulation of the *Cyropaedia*, there is no record of any reader

60. Cf. Plato *Laws* 694a–696a.
61. "εὐθὺς ... εὐθὺς," 8.8.2. Cf. *Mem.* 3.5.5–18. Sage 1994,167–68, points out the nice ambiguity that follows from the description of Cyrus caring for his subjects as if they were his children: "The *paides* here could refer to his subjects as well as his sons.... We do not see Cyrus acting as a father to his sons anywhere in the *Cyropaedia*."
62. Cf. Higgins 1977, 57; Tatum 1989, 220–21.

finding the last chapter at odds with all that comes before it or objecting to its inclusion as an obvious interpolation by some other hand. Not until the beginning of the nineteenth century did philologists start to raise questions concerning the coherence between the final chapter and the body of the work. Their objections essentially boil down to two. First, if one assumes that Xenophon's purpose in the *Cyropaedia* is to present an idealized portrait of a perfect prince to be admired and imitated as a positive example, then the final chapter undercuts the practical efficacy of such a model. Second, it seems impossible that one and the same mind could have composed what is taken to be a glowing and favorable account of Persia together with one of the most venomous anti-Persian diatribes in all of Greek literature.[63] The various attempts to account for these perceived difficulties have generally divided modern commentators into two schools of interpretation. The first resolves the problem in the simplest and most straightforward manner possible by denying that Xenophon wrote the final chapter. One of the most forceful exponents of this position is Walter Miller, the translator of the Loeb edition. He prefaces the offending chapter with the following note:

Chapter VIII can be considered only as a later addition to Xenophon's work—a bit of historical criticism in a review accompanying the book reviewed. It spoils the perfect unity of the work up to this chapter: Cyrus is born, grows to manhood, completes his conquests, establishes his kingdom, organizes the various departments of his empire, dies. Some violent opponent of Medic influence in Athens could not leave all this glorification of Persian institutions unchallenged, and so in this appendix he has supplied an account of the degeneracy of the descendants of the virtuous Persians of the earlier day. The chapter is included here in accord with all the manuscripts and editions. But the reader is recommended to close the book at this point and read no further.

Even if one were to grant the already doubtful premise that Xenophon was concerned with "the perfect unity of the work," at least as unity is understood by Miller, this would only strengthen the case for inclusion of the chapter. After all, the *Cyropaedia* does not begin with Cyrus's birth but rather with Xenophon's reflections on political instability

---

63. See Tatum 1989, 220–25, for an account of the origins and development of this approach.

and his wonder at Cyrus's achievement. For the book to close with Xenophon's considered judgment of that achievement, with particular regard to its stability, can hardly be considered a mark against the unity of its structure. More important, however, Miller ignores the significant transformation the Persians undergo over the course of the book, from austere republican citizens to imperial subjects.

Those who subscribe to Miller's solution cite earlier technical studies disputing Xenophon's authorship of the chapter on stylistic grounds.[64] But, as Tatum points out, these philologists had their own scholarly agendas and were frequently "inclined to look for discrepancies, and if necessary, to invent them where none had existed before."[65] Today, classicists almost universally accept Gustav Eichler's conclusion that on considerations of style, there are no reasons to doubt, and many indications to confirm, Xenophon's authorship of the final chapter.[66] But this consensus creates its own problems. If Xenophon did write the final chapter, how are we to explain its opposition to the rest of the work? Here a second school of interpretation emerges with commentators like Bodil Due, James Tatum, and Deborah Gera, who posit simplistic rhetorical strategies and elaborate psychological theories to account for the book's incoherence, tracing its origin ultimately to what they take to be the incoherence of Xenophon's mind. Others, like Franco Ferrari, simply ascribe the problem to Xenophon's carelessness and failure to make a much-needed final revision.[67] On the whole, these theories have more to say about the techniques and themes of twentieth-century literary criticism than they do about the intentions of our author. As Tatum notes in good postmodern and self-deprecating fashion, "An enduring characteristic of those of us engaged in philology or literary criticism is our ability to discover solutions to problems we have ourselves invented."[68]

I hope to have shown in the analysis above what earlier readers were better able to perceive: namely, that the contradiction between the last chapter and the rest of the work is only apparent. Throughout the whole of book 8 of the *Cyropaedia,* and in several places well

64. E.g., Bornemann 1819, Linke 1874; cf. Eichler 1880, 1–5, Cobet 1875, 66–72.
65. Tatum 1989, 222.
66. Eichler 1880.
67. Ferrari 1995, 783.
68. Tatum 1989, 223.

before, Xenophon shows that the seeds of the swift disintegration of Cyrus's empire are sown with its foundation. The final chapter in no way detracts from the essential unity and coherence of the work. Rather, it confirms it by making explicit the direction of the implicit movement and argument conveyed throughout.[69] This is not to say that the shock modern readers have felt is entirely misplaced. Xenophon intends the ending to surprise the naive and enthusiastic admirer of Cyrus and of empire, to produce in him a sense of wonder followed by a realization of the necessity to return to the beginning and reexamine the whole in the light cast by its conclusion. There is absolutely nothing in the *Cyropaedia* to suggest that its author wished or thought its meaning to be apparent on a single, cursory reading, while there is much in both its contents and peculiar narrative structure to indicate the contrary. Indeed, Xenophon begins his explicit instruction of the reader only in the final chapter (8.8.2),[70] although as early as 1.2.15 he states that clarity requires (re)examining what has come before in the light of what comes after. In practice, this demands rereading.

What is necessary today is to reconsider and overturn the unexamined assumptions that have commonly been applied to the analysis and interpretation of Xenophon's intention in the work. For not only is the swift collapse of the empire foreseeable, but in almost every case the particular defects Xenophon relates can be traced directly back to the practices and institutions established by his so-called "perfect prince." In the last sentence of the final chapter, Xenophon claims to have demonstrated that "the Persians and their associates have become more impious regarding the gods, more irreverent regarding relatives, more unjust regarding others, and more unmanly in what pertains to war than were their predecessors" (8.8.27). According to Gera, the great defect in Cyrus's institutions is that their success requires his enlightened and benevolent management. His death is the cause of the collapse.[71] Xenophon, however, seems to consider his death at most a catalyst or trigger. Nowhere does he identify it as a cause.

---

69. Like Too 1998, 287–89, I see no reason to resort to what she objects to as "reading between the lines" in order to make sense of the *Cyropaedia*, especially in order to see how the final chapter forms an integral part of the whole. Attention to the details of the text suffices.

70. Too 1998, 302.

71. Gera 1993, 297–98.

According to him, the Persians' impiety manifests itself most clearly in their willingness to break their solemn oaths. When he explains the cause of this, as well as of their irreverence toward relatives, he makes no mention of Cyrus's absence. Rather, he cites the behavior of Mithridatas and Rheomithres. These men betrayed fathers, wives, and children and transgressed "the greatest oaths," all in order to do something advantageous for the king, for in this way they would be rewarded with "the greatest honors" (8.8.2–5). Yet this willingness to place service to the king before that to family and gods was already in evidence during Cyrus's reign (8.1.24; 8.2.9). Moreover, it is the logical and predictable result of his policy of weakening family ties by the magnanimity of his gifts and of honoring those who please him regardless of their virtues (8.1.29; 8.4.5; 8.1.25).

To demonstrate the Persians' decline in justice, Xenophon cites two other practices. First, the property of the rich is subjected to arbitrary seizure, so that they live in as much fear of punishment as those who commit many injustices. Second, the children no longer attend schools of justice where they hear cases being decided justly, but instead see disputes settled though the use of bribes (8.8.6, 13). Both of these practices can be traced directly back to Cyrus. Confiscations were not unknown in his day, nor could anyone consider his property secure once this ruler began to regard his subjects as indistinguishable from his treasury. As for the disappearance of the schools of justice, they are neither necessary nor possible once Cyrus himself becomes a "seeing law." And, as we have seen, the courts that Cyrus allows to operate are designed by him to stir up the mutual envy of his subjects in a manner that also encourages the practice of bribery, not justice (8.1.20, 22; 8.2.27–28).[72]

According to Xenophon, this increase in injustice leads to a decline in manliness and military virtue, making the Persians unwilling to associate with the strong or join the army (8.8.6). As for their impiety, which in Xenophon's account calls forth no divine punishment, it further undermines the mutual trust and confidence that contributed to their earlier successes (8.8.7). Overeating and drinking, less frequent hunting expeditions, and a taste for Median luxuries also take their toll on the Persians' bodily strength and endurance. This enervation

72. For the acquisition of φιλία through money, see 8.2.2.

manifests itself in a passionate devotion to culinary arts and innovations and the pursuit of soft beds and carpets, as well as various contrivances to avoid subjecting themselves to extremes of heat and cold. But it is Cyrus who first introduces his men to refined cooking (8.2.5–7), clothes them in Median dress (8.3.1), cuts back on the number of hunting expeditions (8.1.37–38), and sets the example of pursuing a perpetual spring by moving about his empire with the change of seasons (8.6.22).[73] Most disastrously, the Persians are simply no longer willing to fight, although they still possess and carry the weapons for engaging an enemy at close quarters (8.8.23–25). The most compelling explanation of this comes from the mouth of Cyrus himself. Early in the campaign against the Assyrians, he explains his refusal to follow Chrysantas's suggestion that he exhort the troops before going into battle as the Assyrian had done:

Could a single spoken word all at once fill the souls of those who hear it with respect, or avert them from what is shameful; or convince them that they must take on every labor and every risk for the sake of praise, and impress it firmly on their minds that they must rather choose to die in battle than to save themselves in flight? If such thoughts are to be inscribed in men and remain abiding, must there not first be such laws that will provide an honored and free life for the good and impose a wretched life, grievous and not worth living, on the bad? Next, there must surely be teachers and rulers over them who will correctly show, teach, and habituate them to do these things until it is inbred in them to believe in reality (τῷ ὄντι νομίζειν) that the good and renowned are most happy, and to hold that the bad and ill-famed are most wretched of all. For such ought to be the instruction of those who are going to show that learning is stronger than fear of the enemy. (3.3.51–53)

This speech, delivered just before a battle won by the virtue of men raised and educated under Persian laws, demonstrates that Cyrus knows the political requirements or conditions necessary for military excellence. His abject failure to reproduce these conditions, whether altogether intentional or merely a consequence of unforeseen constraints imposed by the necessities governing his empire, accounts for the unwillingness to fight of those brought up under his rule. Armed as he is with this knowledge, Cyrus must know that the political virtue of his subjects is suffering and will dramatically decline with the passing

73. Cf. 6.2.29, *Mem.* 4.3.8–9, *Oec.* 17.4; Dio Chrysostom *Discourse VI* 1–12.

of his own Persian-bred generation. The conquest of the known world happens to coincide with this moment and brings his policy of expansion to an end,[74] eliminating both his greatest source of revenue and the presence of a common external enemy.[75] In light of the overwhelming difficulties created by the disappearance of these irreplaceable props, it seems unlikely that even Cyrus could have kept the empire from collapse.

Cyrus is a man who enjoys to an uncommon degree the apparent favor of the gods. Perhaps nothing attests to this so much as the timeliness of his death, just when he considers himself to have reached the height of his powers, that is, just when even he would have faced an inevitable decline (8.7.6). A dream comes to him one night in which "something more than human seemed to him to approach and say, 'Get ready, Cyrus, for you are already going away to the gods'" (8.7.2). One could perhaps take this dream to be the last piece of evidence bearing witness to the benevolent care the gods have taken of him throughout his life. Cyrus, however, interprets it in a much different manner. He questions both its veracity and divine origin. Xenophon relates that when he awakes the next morning, he is "almost" certain his death is at hand; later, he speaks of the prediction conditionally; and, finally, in contradiction to the implied promise of the more-than-human messenger, he expresses doubts about the immortality of the soul (8.7.2, 8, 27). Cyrus even suggests that he considers the message to be more than likely the product of his own mind: "Consider that nothing human is nearer to death than sleep; then the soul of a human being appears most divine and foresees something of what is to come; for it is likely that it is then most free" (8.7.21). It is perhaps for this reason that Cyrus omits all mention of the dream when he explains to those gathered around him how he knows that his life is now coming

74. In order to emphasize the connection between the political consequences of world conquest and Cyrus's policies, Xenophon anachronistically exaggerates the extent of the Persian empire and attributes to Cyrus several of his successors' conquests (1.1.4–5, 8.6.21, 8.8.1). See Baron de Sainte-Croix, "Nouvelles observations sur la Cyropédie," in Schneider 1800, 551 ff.

75. In all of Xenophon's writings, the "common good" of any political community is inseparable from, if not entirely constituted by, the presence of hostile or potential enemies. See 1.2.2 with 1.2.15, 1.6.27–30, and 2.1.3, 1.5.8, 3.3.10, 4.5.32, 5.3.23, 5.5.19; *Ages.* 7.7; *CL* 11.1 with 13.6, 6.3; *Anab.* 3.1.46; *Oec.* 3.15, 7.12; *Hel.* 6.5.34; *Hiero* 11.1 with 7.12. Cf. *Mem.* 1.6.13–15.

to an end (8.7.6). In Xenophon's account, it proves to be as difficult to distinguish between what the dream seems to counsel and what Cyrus in his own considered judgment thinks is best, as it is to distinguish between the counsels of the mysterious *daimonion* of Socrates and the philosopher's own deliberations on his end.[76] One thing, however, is clear: Cyrus's decision to abstain from food is entirely his own (8.7.4; cf. 1.6.9). To the list of similarities often noted between the deaths of Cyrus and Socrates,[77] it seems that we must add yet another. Both appear to have picked the moment at least in part to avoid suffering certain future ills.[78] It is difficult to fault Cyrus for making this timely exit, but the character of the empire he leaves behind compels us to reject the accepted view that his policies represent, or were intended by Xenophon to represent, an ideal for imitation.[79]

76. *Apol.* 1, 4–8, 23, 27.

77. Luccioni 1953, 149–50; Gera 1993, 129–30.

78. *Mem.* 4.8.1; *Apol.* 1, 27, 33.

79. Strauss 1968, 193: "If Xenophon was not a fool, he did not intend to present Cyrus's regime as a model. He knew too well that the good order of society requires stability and continuity." Too 1998, 288, 301, follows Strauss's judgment. See Introduction, n. 8, above.

Chapter Four

Motives

In the *Hiero*, Xenophon shows that the tyrant is motivated above all by a desire to be loved, and, as he also remains deeply attached to his fatherland, to be loved by his fellow countrymen.[1] Tyrannical power appears to be the path to this love, because it puts him in a position to do great favors; and "by nature all believe that they love those by whom they believe they are benefited."[2] Yet there are limits to the beneficence that a ruler can exercise. In particular, as Xenophon openly admits in the much more candid *Hiero*, the tyrant must commit various irregular or criminal acts not simply to acquire but also to preserve his rule: above all, he must expel, enslave, or otherwise make sure of the brave, the wise, and the just.[3] The desire to be loved by all subjects cannot be satisfied through the exercise of tyrannical power, however, and Simonides therefore exhorts Hiero to concern himself less with being loved and instead with being admired and praised. Admiration, depending more on his qualities than services, could plausibly be bestowed on him by those he does not directly benefit, perhaps even by some whom he must harm. And if a ruler is most admired for making his city happy, a change in orientation such as Simonides suggests might contribute to the amelioration of the lives of Hiero's subjects as well.[4]

Cyrus, like any actual ruler, wishes to be loved by his subjects. He even ranks this among "the most important things" (1.6.24). Yet he appears to desire their love more as a means of obtaining their

---

1. *Hiero* 3.5; 5.3; 8.1; 11.8. Strauss 1968, 58, 82.
2. *Oec.* 20.29; cf. *Hel.* 7.3.12.
3. *Hiero* 5.1–2.
4. *Hiero* 11.1–12. Strauss 1968, 91, 93.

faithful obedience than as something to be pursued for its own sake. Unlike Hiero, he never claims that love is something sweet or pleasant in itself (1.6.26; 5.1.12; 7.5.59; *Hiero* 3.3). Rather, Cyrus appears "to have endured every labor and faced every risk for the sake of praise" (1.2.1). His desire for praise does not, of course, exclude all other passions. Like the other men of whom he has experience, he remains insatiable in his desire for wealth (8.2.20).[5] But he also knows that a superabundance of money and other material goods brings troubles of its own. These things must be counted, weighed, and cleaned; they either spoil or must be guarded with great care. "Glory (εὔκλεια), however, to the extent that there is more, becomes greater, nobler, and lighter to bear; it often, too, makes those who bear it lighter" (8.2.22). Cyrus's fundamental concern with praise, then, marks him as the kind of ruler who seems to know how to get the most satisfaction from his rule without the assistance of a teacher. As we have already noted, many of the suggestions that Simonides makes to Hiero about how to improve his rule are implemented by Cyrus on his own initiative. This is not to say that Simonides could teach Cyrus nothing of utility. Some of the advice that he gives to Hiero could also have been heeded with profit by Cyrus. For instance, in their passionate love of victory, both rulers make the mistake of continuing to compete against mere private men (πρὸς ἰδιώτας): Hiero, by outfitting chariots; Cyrus, by riding in a horse race with his Persian subjects. Losing would expose both to severe (if not open) ridicule, while victory can earn them only envy.[6] Cyrus wins his race, and even defeats the other Persians "by far," but the victory is hollow. For who would be so foolish as to beat such a master?

More generally, this difficulty must also taint the pleasure Cyrus takes in being honored by his subjects. Much as Hiero's tyranny over his city makes it next to impossible for him to distinguish between genuine and false love even or especially among those whom he favors,[7] Cyrus's position in his empire makes it hard for him to distinguish between genuine and false praise (8.1.16–20; 8.2.12; 8.6.23).[8] This problem was

5. Cf. 1.6.45; *Oec.* 1.14, *Poroi* 4.7.
6. Cf. *Anab.* 1.9.24.
7. *Hiero* 1.37–38.
8. Cf. *Hiero* 7.5–8.

already present in his earlier praise of tyranny. Those who are serious about praise do not desire tyranny simply in order to be in a position to do great benefactions; nor do they seek such power only to establish an objective superiority over their fellows. Rather, Cyrus maintains, the lover of honor is drawn to tyranny by the freedom it apparently bestows; above all, the freedom from external restraints that alone makes it possible to manifest his "goodwill," to demonstrate that he holds back from unjust and impious acts independent of compulsion, considerations of policy, or other material gain. Power shows the man. Absolute power, far from corrupting, shows the man completely. By stripping bare the motives, it becomes the sine qua non of praise for what one genuinely is. Thus Cyrus claims that he would not trade all the wealth of Babylon, "no, not even of all the world," for the opportunity that Gobryas gives him to show his own true colors (5.2.9–12).

Yet Cyrus's praise of tyranny is itself highly colored. If the omnipotence and freedom of one necessarily precludes that of all others, the conditions for revealing one's true self preclude the expression of a disinterested judgment. Moreover, no human being is ever likely to find himself in a position in which he is entirely free "to make clear" what sort of man he is (cf. 1.6.46). Certainly, no ruler could ever do so (7.5.37; 8.1.40–41).[9] Nor is it in fact the case when Gobryas surrenders his fort. Cyrus's honorable treatment of this defector is a stroke of good policy, one calculated to win him other much-needed allies. And later, even when at the height of his power, he remains bound to control the vast majority of his subjects by compulsion and deceit (1.1.5; 5.2.19; 7.5.37; 8.3.14; 8.7.7, 28) . The closer Cyrus approaches his goal of ruling the world, the further the satisfaction of genuine praise recedes. But perhaps the complete domination of his age, while casting a regrettable shadow on the praise (and blame) it can offer, provides the surest path to that greater immortality of fame bestowed by future, disinterested generations, who, standing at a safe distance, will not be similarly compromised.[10] Yet Cyrus is far from certain that he will be in a position to enjoy his posthumous glory (8.7.22).[11] Nor can he feel his

9. Cf. Plato *Republic* 414b–d, 382e–383a.
10. Cf. Thucydides 2.63–64.
11. Cicero *De Senectute* 23.82: "Were it not the case that souls are immortal, those of the best men would not strive for immortal glory." Cf. 22.81; *De Divinatione* 2.58.119.

reputation will be altogether safe from the envy or achievements of those who come after him. Cyrus anticipates the ambition of those whom he considers to be most likely to surpass him in future times by setting them one against the other through the division of his kingdom. If someone admitted to be a tyrant by his own daughter can come to be remembered as a king (1.2.1; 1.3.18), the opposite can surely happen too. To secure the sanctity of his memory against those who might later vilify him, Cyrus must invoke a general fear of the gods who have seemed so much to favor him. And insofar as he imagines, or wishes others to imagine, the condition of his soul in the afterlife, it is as a spirit taking vengeance on those who fail to show his name a proper reverence (8.7.18–22, 8).

Cyrus not only pursues honor and wealth himself, but inspires others to make these their aims as well (1.5.9; 4.2.44). Although his own ambitions limit the scope of his followers' achievements, in certain respects they are in a better position to enjoy and profit from their efforts. No one responds to his call with more enthusiasm, or finds himself so happy with the imperial order Cyrus establishes, than Pheraulus. Yet the conditions that make for his satisfaction are not those that govern Cyrus's life. Although Pheraulus considers a life of honor to be the most pleasant life of all, even he is willing to follow it only when he believes there is a disinterested judge to award each according to his merits; and he trusts that Cyrus will be such a one (2.3.11–12).[12] Cyrus, however, can trust no one to treat him disinterestedly. As for the satisfactions of wealth, here, too, Pheraulus finds himself in something of a better position to enjoy them. He soon discovers what Cyrus already knows, namely, that the possession of too much wealth turns out to be more trouble than it is worth. Pheraulus complains to an unnamed Sacian who is much impressed by his riches:

Do you suppose, Sacian, that I now eat, drink, and sleep in any way more pleasantly than back when I was poor? As to there being more, here is what I gain: I need to guard more, to distribute more to others, and to have the trouble of taking care of more. For now, of course, many servants demand

---

12. Pheraulus himself seems inclined to act on quite a different principle when in charge of distributing goods, although not without some justification, indeed, the same justification that excuses so many of Cyrus's apparent departures from strict justice (8.3.7–8).

food of me, many drink, and many demand clothes. Others need doctors, and someone else comes in carrying either sheep that have been mangled by wolves, or with cattle that have fallen off cliffs, or professing that disease has fallen over the flocks. Consequently, I think that I am in more pain now because I have many things than I was before because I had few.... And having money is not so pleasant as losing it is painful.... And doubtless there is a necessity, Sacian, that he who has much also spend much on the gods, on friends, and on guests. So whoever is intensely pleased by money, be assured that he also feels intense pain upon spending it. (8.3.40–44)[13]

Despite Pheraulus's speech, the Sacian remains unmoved in his conviction that happiness consists in both having more and spending more. Yet their complementary disagreement provides the basis on which the two establish a household for the mutual benefit of each. Pheraulus takes charge of acquiring and bringing home the wealth, while the Sacian rules over and cares for it (8.3.45–48).[14] The Sacian is altogether surprised at his partner's willingness to enter into this arrangement. But Xenophon explains that Pheraulus possesses a congenial character and nothing seems so pleasant or beneficial to him as to serve human beings. The reason for this is that he considers man "to be the best of the animals and the most grateful," that is, willing to return another's good service (ἀντιθεραπεύειν) and praise independent of any calculation of future goods (8.3.49; cf. 1.1.2; 1.2.7). Thus Pheraulus surrenders the care and burden of rule because he believes he will suffer no harm and even benefit himself by doing so. Yet his view of the world rests on fundamental misconceptions.[15] For instance, he mistakes the combined workings of chance and Cyrus's whimsy for evidence of the gods' providential care.[16] While he may believe that his partner cares for him out of gratitude for his past services, Xenophon informs the reader that the Sacian in fact "loved Pheraulus because he was always bringing in something more" (8.3.50). If Pheraulus escapes the burden of rule and comes to no harm by abandoning it, he owes his safety less to the natural goodness of man than to his being the king's close con-

13. Cf. 8.2.20; *Oec.* 7.2.3.
14. Cf. *Oec.* 7.35–36.
15. Xenophon stresses the subjective character of both Pheraulus's and the Sacian's happiness (ἡγεῖτο εὐδαίμων ... ἐνομίζει μακαριώτατος, 8.3.48).
16. τυγχάνει ... ἔτυχε, 8.3.28, 32.

fidant (8.3.7; 8.4.2). His happiness is possible only in the world as
Cyrus, not the gods or nature, has ordered it.[17] Cyrus, however, considers man to be naturally inclined to ingratitude (8.2.27; 8.7.16; cf.
1.6.32; 1.2–3, 7) and does not appear to place his trust in a divine,
or at least beneficent, natural order (2.2.27; 5.2.12; 7.1.11; 8.2.20;
8.6.22, with 6.2.29).[18] When Croesus volunteers to serve Cyrus in
the same capacity as Pheraulus's Sacian, the offer is refused, and
Cyrus keeps him under close watch as a possible threat (7.2.27–29;
8.3.47). As the source or enforcer of order, Cyrus cannot trust to
that order to diminish the burden of his rule. His satisfactions must
accordingly suffer.

Love

The *Cyropaedia* is the founding document of a genre that came to be
known as "mirrors of princes." For the most part, it treats political
life on its own terms and analyzes it in the light cast by its own
principles, clarifying their implications on the assumption that politics
is both the first and most important concern of man. Yet Xenophon
devotes a considerable portion of the work (roughly seven of its forty-
one chapters) to relating the passionate if connubial love story of
Panthea and Abradatas. The *Cyropaedia* is also, then, among the
founding documents of the genre "romance novel," a species of writing
whose emergence is usually associated with a radical deprecation of
the political sphere of life. The very presence of this story, which
has contributed considerably to the book's most memorable scenes,[19]
certainly highlights Cyrus's own deprecation of the passion of love and
his indifference to the charms of "the most beautiful woman in Asia"
(5.2.7–9; 8.4.22; 8.5.28).[20]

The essentials of Panthea's story are as follows. She is captured early
in the war when her husband happens to be away on a diplomatic
mission to Bactria. In dividing up the spoils, the allies naturally set her
aside for Cyrus (4.6.11; 5.1.3). He, in turn, assigns Araspas, a Mede

17. Cf. 6.1.41. Compare a similar confusion on the part of Socrates' companion
Hermogenes (*Symp.* 4.48–50 with *Mem.* 2.10). Bartlett 1996, 193–94.
18. Cf. *Oec.* 21.22.
19. Grant 1872, 141; Tatum 1989, 21–28.
20. Bruell 1969, 128–29.

and companion of his youth, to watch over her. When this man praises her beauty and bids Cyrus to go and take a look himself, he refuses with an oath:

"No, by Zeus, and all the less [shall I go] if she really is such as you say."
"Why so?" said the youth.
"Because," he said, "if hearing from you that she is beautiful persuades me to go to look upon her, even though at the moment I do not have much leisure, I fear that she herself will persuade me much more readily to look again. Consequently, I would perhaps sit there gazing at her to the neglect of what I need to do."
Then the youth laughed and said, "Cyrus, do you consider the beauty of a human being to be sufficient to compel someone against his will to act contrary to what is best? If, indeed, this were so by nature, all would be similarly compelled. Do you see how fire burns all alike? For it is so by nature. But concerning beautiful things, they love some but not others; and one loves one, another [loves] another. For it depends on the will, and each loves what he wishes. For example, a brother does not love his sister, but another [loves] her. For fear and law are sufficient to prevent love. But if a law were set down [forbidding] those who do not eat to be hungry, or those who do not drink to be thirsty, or against being cold in the winter or hot in the summer, no such law would have the power to make human beings obey. For they are by nature overpowered by such things. But to love is a matter of the will. At any rate, each loves what suits him, just as with clothes or shoes."
"How then," said Cyrus, "if love is a matter of the will, is it not possible to stop when one wishes? But I have seen people weeping from the pain of love, and enslaved to those they love, even though before they fell in love they believed slavery to be very evil. And they give away many things it would be better not to part with. They even pray to be delivered from it, just as with some disease. Yet, unable to get free, they are bound by a necessity stronger than iron. At any rate, they surrender themselves to serve the beloved heedlessly and in many things. And yet, in spite of suffering from these ills, they do not even try to run away, but stand guard lest those they love run off." (5.1.8–12)

Undaunted by Cyrus's fears, Araspas confidently assures him that "even if I never stop gazing [at Panthea] I shall not be so overcome as to do anything I ought not to do." Cyrus, however, continues to steer clear of Panthea himself. But he does allow his comrade to remain as her guard and enjoins him to take good care of her, "for perhaps this woman might come to turn a timely profit for us" (5.1.17).

With the passage of time, Araspas is seized and altogether captured by love and of necessity is compelled to speak to Panthea of a union (περὶ συνουσίας). She refuses out of loyalty to her absent husband, at which he threatens to take her against her will by force. Only then does she send her eunuch to Cyrus to let him know what is happening. When Araspas finds out that his threats have become known, he is overcome by shame and fears that he will suffer something terrible at Cyrus's hands. Making the most of this public breech between them, Cyrus secretly forgives his comrade and sends him among the Assyrians as a spy.[21] There he gains admission on the pretext that he is fleeing some terrible punishment. When Panthea learns that she has been the cause of Cyrus losing a valuable friend, she writes her husband to defect to the Persian camp. Abradatas becomes a devoted follower of Cyrus's, and on the eve of the last pitched battle, he volunteers to position his chariot against the strongest part of the enemy line. As he is putting on his usual armor, Panthea brings out a golden helmet, armlets, bracelets, a long purple tunic, and a plume dyed dark red. She has had these things made without her husband's knowledge and has paid for them by selling her own jewelry. Yet this sacrifice is nothing compared to that which she is prepared to make: "If any other woman ever valued her husband more than her own life, I think you know that I, too, am such a one.... Still, with the affection that you know me to have for you, I nevertheless swear to you on my love and yours that I would rather be put under the earth in common with you, when you have been a good man, than live in shame with one who has been shamed, so worthy of what is most noble have I deemed both you and myself"(6.4.5–6).[22] Encouraged by her words, Abradatas leads his companions against the great mass of the enemy, where they are cut down and perish to a man (7.1.30–32). In the aftermath of the battle, Panthea has his corpse taken up and brought to a hill near the river for burial. There Cyrus finds her grieving with the head of the mutilated corpse cradled in her lap.[23] He grasps the right hand of Abradatas, but it comes away in his, having been cut off with a sword:

21. Cf. *Hipparchicus* 4.7–8.
22. Panthea's speech stands in defiance to the sentiments expressed by Achilles' shade in Hades, although she soon comes to echo some of the dead hero's regrets (Homer *Odyssey* 11.487–491; cf. *Iliad* 9.315–418).
23. Cf. Homer *Iliad* 24.724.

And the woman wailed and taking the hand back from Cyrus kissed it and attached it again as best she could, and said, "The rest is like this also, Cyrus. But why must you see it? And I know that he suffered this not least because of me, and perhaps also no less because of you, Cyrus. For being foolish, I encouraged him many times to act in such a way that he might become a worthy friend to you. And I myself know that he did not have in mind what he would suffer but what he could do that would [show] his gratitude to you. Accordingly, he himself has died a blameless death, but I who was exhorting him sit beside him alive." (7.3.10)

Cyrus assures her that in fact Abradatas had met "the noblest end" and promises her safe passage to wherever she might wish to go (7.3.1; cf. 7.1.19; 8.1.48). As soon as Panthea is left alone she takes a sword and stabs herself, placing her head on her husband's chest to die in his cold embrace. Her eunuchs then draw their swords and kill themselves (7.3.14–15).

On reading these passages from the *Cyropaedia*, Plutarch was moved to wonder, "Who could find greater pleasure in sleeping with the most beautiful woman than in sitting up with Xenophon's story of Panthea?"[24] Indeed, the pleasure we take in contemplating the depth and passion of such mutual devotion threatens to eclipse whatever admiration we may have for the prosaic and calculating virtues of Cyrus (6.4.11; 8.5.18–20, 28). The tragedy of Panthea and Abradatas draws attention to the cold, unerotic, and perhaps even truncated nature of Cyrus's soul, and reminds the reader of a dimension of human experience outside the range of his proper activities as a ruler.

Yet it would be a mistake to think this pursuit of a romantic and self-sacrificing love makes Panthea and Abradatas superior to Cyrus in Xenophon's eyes. For one thing, their ideal depends too much for the intensity of its charms upon the political sphere it might otherwise seem to transcend to offer a genuine alternative. Panthea and Abradatas's love thrives on its public character, and their desire to be together is strictly limited by considerations of appearance. Panthea sends for her husband only when there is an honorable and publicly known occasion for him to defect from the Assyrian camp. When they do at last meet again they embrace but then immediately turn to a

24. Plutarch *That Epicurus Makes a Pleasant Life Impossible* 1093c.

discussion of Cyrus and his many virtues.[25] Before the final battle, Panthea takes great trouble over Abradatas's appearance. "For you will be my greatest ornament *if you appear also to others* as you do to me" (6.4.3; emphasis added). And Abradatas prays to Zeus that he might "show himself worthy" of such a wife. To do so he vies for the most dangerous and prominent position in the ranks of the allies (6.4.9; 6.3.35; 7.1.15–16). His final appearance as a corpse unfit to be seen brings home the "effectual truth" of their shared understanding of nobility, to say nothing of its consequences for their loyal servants and companions (7.1.30–31; 7.3.15). One might think the horrible sight of her husband's mutilated body would cause Panthea to repudiate her earlier aspirations.[26] But this would be to exaggerate the extent to which the brutality of Abradatas's end comes as a genuine surprise to her. She may rail against the folly of having encouraged his boldness and profess her ignorance of what he would ultimately suffer, but she has clearly and with some calculation anticipated the scene that she now stages. Xenophon tells us that Panthea had "long ago prepared" the sword with which she takes her life; and when her eunuchs follow suit, they do so only after having positioned themselves "where she had [previously] ordered" (7.3.14–15). To the end she remains intent on playing out a part she has imagined and rehearsed.

Panthea can embrace the fate toward which she knows or suspects her love of Abradatas leads because she believes that their self-sacrifice will be much remarked and long remembered, a belief her husband also shares. But insofar as this hope depends on their trust in the benevolent care of Cyrus, it is, like Pheraulus's belief in the goodness of human nature, ill-founded. From the beginning, Panthea mistakes the character of Cyrus's interest in and care for her. When Araspas begins to court her, she hesitates to inform Cyrus, assuming that were Araspas's advances to become known, it would set the two friends at odds. Not until Araspas threatens to rape her does she make known her plight. Cyrus's first response on hearing of this development is to laugh at Araspas, who professed himself to be "stronger than love." He then sends someone to tell Araspas "not to use violence with such a

25. Cf. ὥσπερ εἰκὸς ... ἀνεπαύοντο σὺν ἀλλήλοις at 3.1.41 with ἠσπάζοντο ἀλλήλους ... ὡς εἰκὸς at 6.1.47.

26. Gera 1993, 239, 241.

woman, but if he could persuade her, he [Cyrus] would not stand in the way." It is not Cyrus but the messenger, Artabazus, who takes it upon himself to rebuke Araspas, "calling the woman a sacred trust and telling him of his impiety, injustice, and lack of continence" (6.1.34–35). Although Cyrus makes good use of Araspas's terrified response and fear of punishment, he in no way blames him for his actions.[27] If Panthea wishes to send for her husband in order to recompense her protector for the apparent loss of his friend, there is no reason for him to correct her mistaken impression. From his wife, Abradatas hears only of Cyrus's "piety, moderation, and pity toward herself," and, like a gentleman, he thinks above all of how to repay him. On the eve of the great battle, Panthea again reminds her husband:

And I think we owe Cyrus some great favor, because when I was a captive and had been selected for him, he did not think it worthy to possess me either as a slave or as a free woman under a dishonorable name, but he guarded me for you as if he had taken his brother's wife. And in addition, when Araspas, the one who was watching over me, defected, I promised him that if he would allow me to send to you, you would come to him, a man much more loyal and better. (6.4.7–8)

To this Abradatas responds, "Greatest Zeus, allow me to show myself as a husband worthy of Panthea and a friend worthy of Cyrus who has honored us." Whatever else the two may have imagined of Cyrus, we must note that he never expresses the slightest concern for Panthea's honor; and far from keeping her as a brother's wife, he sees nothing wrong in Araspas sleeping with her. Moreover, it is this very Araspas, not Abradatas, whom he publicly declares to be "the best man" (6.3.15). Panthea and Abradatas die in complete ignorance that Cyrus has dealt with them from start to finish solely on the basis of political expediency (5.1.17). They, if not the reader, would be surprised to learn that their tomb somehow comes to be known as the Monument of the Eunuchs, a class of subjects of the utmost utility to Cyrus within the empire (7.3.15; 7.5.58–65).

The story of Panthea and Abradatas may be the most prominent love affair related in the *Cyropaedia*, but it is not the only one. Tigranes, "newly married and very much in love with his wife," also expresses his

27. Cf. Romilly 1976, 320.

willingness to sacrifice his life for her, not, however, to make publicly manifest the depth and nobility of his devotion, but to keep her alive and out of captivity (3.1.36). Even in the midst of the enthusiasm and public acclaim for Cyrus's virtues, she, in turn, prefers to look upon "the one who would pay with his own life (ψυχή) so that I not become a slave" (3.1.41). It is perhaps not too much to see in Tigranes' devotion to this woman with a "manly" disposition (8.4.24), in his desire to have her with him always as the true judge of his worth (3.1.43), and in the essentially private character of their love,[28] an image of Xenophon's own quiet devotion to philosophy with the self-sufficient and private satisfactions it confers, and a profession of his own willingness to sacrifice, like his teacher, to keep her alive and free.[29] This interpretation gains some support from an incident already related. We recall that Cyrus refuses even to look upon the beautiful Panthea out of fear that she might persuade him to spend his time gazing upon her rather than attending to his duties (5.1.7–8). This passage must be understood in the light cast by its parallel in the *Memorabilia*. There someone tells Socrates that Theodote, a woman of indescribable beauty, is in Athens. To this he immediately declares, "We must then go and look." Much as Cyrus fears Panthea will do with him, this Theodote tries to persuade Socrates to come and see her often. But he refuses on the thin pretext of having many private and public engagements to attend to, and tells her bluntly that if she were to visit him, he would welcome her only if he found himself with no one dearer.[30] The charms and satisfactions of Socrates' way of life, unlike those of Cyrus, permit him to look upon the beautiful without being swayed from his proper pursuit or activity. He possesses the

---

28. οἴκαδε ... σύν ἀλλήλοις, 3.1.41.

29. For the image of Socrates as a matchmaker for those in love with philosophy, see *Symp.* 4.62; cf. *Mem.* 3.11.17–18. For the nature of Xenophon's "sacrifice," consider Strauss 1939, 536: "[This article] will not have been written in vain if it induces some readers to reconsider the traditional view of Xenophon, which, while being understandable and even to a certain extent justifiable, is almost an insult to this truly royal soul. For such a man was he that he preferred to go through the centuries in the disguise of a beggar rather than to sell the precious secrets of Socrates' quiet and sober wisdom to a multitude which let him escape to immortality only after he had intoxicated it by his artful stories of the swift and dazzling actions of an Agesilaus or a Cyrus, or a Xenophon."

30. *Mem.* 3.11.

equanimity born of true moderation, whereas Cyrus remains merely continent, apparently divided between his political duties and the inclinations of his soul.[31]

Xenophon orchestrates this comparison between Socrates and Cyrus in order to bring out the greater psychic unity of the philosophic life as opposed to the life devoted to conventional or political virtue. It is the Xenophontic parallel to Plato's Myth of Er.[32] Yet, when taken in the context of the *Cyropaedia* as a whole, Cyrus's refusal to look upon Panthea and his struggle to overcome the natural impulse to look upon "the most beautiful woman in Asia" in order to uphold his political duties, might not have posed a genuine dilemma. First, we note that Cyrus chooses Araspas to guard over Panthea because he is someone known to him since childhood (5.1.2–3; cf. 1.4.26), and he perhaps suspects that his own confession of weakness and fear will encourage this companion to surpass his master by proving stronger than her beauty. And if Cyrus really does fear Panthea, he is not troubled enough to banish her from the camp altogether in order to prevent himself or any others from falling victim to her "corruptions." Rather, he hopes that by keeping her, he may gain some timely profit, a policy that bears fruit in the valuable military intelligence he manages to obtain as a consequence of Araspas's public disgrace.[33] When Araspas falls, Cyrus considers himself to be the cause of his comrade's misfortune (αἴτιος, 6.1.36); and Xenophon relates that the whole affair was being managed (ἐπράττετο, 5.1.18).[34] Of course, the mere fact that Cyrus may have gained some political advantage through the skillful manipulation of his boyhood companion is not incompatible with the sincerity of his claim to fear and flee the beautiful. But he does go to see Panthea of his own free will, and well before the political duties he fears she may cause him to neglect have been discharged. Cyrus "immediately" rushes off to see her when he hears she is grieving over the corpse of Abradatas, whose severed hand he somehow manages to detach in the encounter. And he again hurries to see her after learning that she has stabbed herself and lies dead upon her husband's corpse.

31. Strauss 1968, 135–36; Bruell 1969, 128–30.
32. Plato *Republic* 619b–620d.
33. See καιρός at 5.1.17 and 6.3.21.
34. Consider also the peculiar chronology at 6.1.30 and the way it serves to reinforce the connection between Cyrus's need for a spy and Araspas's difficulties.

Much as Socrates can resist the charms of Theodote by virtue of his experience with yet more beautiful things, perhaps Cyrus can allow himself to look upon Panthea only when in the presence of a what is for him a more attractive sight. Such a cruel twist to Cyrus's soul is compatible with other details that Xenophon relates: namely, his having to be dragged off the battlefield after his first taste of fighting to stop his frenzied gazing at the corpses of the fallen (ἐθεᾶτο, 1.4.24; cf. 1.4.11); and the erotic passion he feels for the blood sport of the hunt (1.4.5).[35] Cyrus may publicly profess that he prefers to display his benevolence rather than his generalship (8.4.8; cf. 8.2.1–2, 20, 8.3.44); but, in private, he admits to taking greater pleasure in the practice of deception than in straightforward dealing (1.6.19).[36] At a less guarded moment, he even goes so far as to include "striking down and killing" among, not the necessary means to victory, but its "rewards" (ἆθλα, 7.1.13; cf. 2.3.10; 3.3.62). So, too, his final words indicate the importance he places on doing others harm: "Remember this last thing from me, that by benefiting your friends you will be able to punish your enemies" (8.7.28). With these few but telling details, Xenophon indicates the level at which the demands of political life can be fully harmonized with the passions of the human soul, or at least with one that seems to have received a lasting impression from the spirit of the Persian laws.

35. This is, I believe, the only erotic impulse Xenophon ascribes to Cyrus. Cf. *Anab*. 1.2.12.

36. Cf. *Anab*. 2.6.22–23.

Chapter Five

Xenophon's Intentions

The interpretation of the *Cyropaedia* that I have offered here is open to an obvious objection. If the empire Cyrus founds is inferior to the republican regime, why does Xenophon hesitate to criticize the one and praise the other in a straightforward and direct manner? To understand the reasons for Xenophon's reticence, this difficulty must be considered from several perspectives. Their full elaboration leads to the heart of Xenophon's intention in the *Cyropaedia*.

Xenophon shows in the *Hellenica* that, for both oligarchic and democratic regimes, the impulse toward imperialism remained a prominent, and, on the whole, pathological feature of Greek political life in the aftermath of the Peloponnesian War. The power of this appeal and the general approval accorded to it by his contemporaries increased both the likelihood that it would ultimately prevail and the danger of speaking out against its leading practitioners. Christopher Tuplin, whose careful study of the *Hellenica* has brought out the anti-imperialist thrust of that work, offers this account of Xenophon's failure there openly to condemn Sparta, the dominant, although by no means the only, imperial power he portrays:

The truth is that no individual Spartan emerges wholly unscathed, and no reader should conclude that Xenophon is offering either Sparta as a whole or a particular group of Spartans as a paradigm for emulation.... [O]ne might ask why, if Xenophon wished to indicate to the Athenians (or anyone else) his view on the bankruptcy of certain contemporary political ideals, he did not do so in the form of a [critical] political pamphlet. The answer is, I think, nothing more exciting than that there were constraints upon his freedom of choice.[1]

1. Tuplin 1993, 165, 167.

Tuplin goes on to speculate that chief among these constraints was a "persisting personal sentiment about Sparta" that held Xenophon back from engaging in "mere vituperation" or singling Sparta out for faults that could just as well have been ascribed to other imperial cities. To criticize Sparta would in all fairness have required him to criticize Athens and Thebes. But, according to Tuplin, "the undertaking of actual research on Athenian or Theban history" would have delayed publication of his manuscript. Moreover, it was simply "not to his taste."[2] Although more nuanced and refined, Tuplin's explanation of Xenophon's silence echoes conventional interpretations that find his alleged pro-Spartan bias to be a product of his economic interests, a lack of intellectual curiosity and discipline, a failure in judgment, or all of these combined.

Neither Tuplin's nor any other of the usual reductionist explanations can be verified by recourse to textual evidence. Nor is there any external evidence to suggest that Xenophon was under pressure to publish or that he disliked "actual research" into Athenian and Theban history. Yet, if we base our conclusions on what he actually wrote, it may still be possible to explain his reticence as a matter of taste, although not the indolent distaste for historical inquiries that Tuplin ascribes to him. In his own name, Xenophon writes that "it is both noble and just, and pious and more pleasant to remember good things rather than the bad."[3] This is not to say that he denies the pleasure of remembering and recording the bad, but it does mean he features it less prominently. Those brought up according to the standards of twentieth-century political discourse understandably mistake this delicacy for obtuseness. But Xenophon also indicates a more tangible reason for his reticence, and one that the experience of twentieth-century politics, to say nothing of life in the academy, ought to predispose us better to understand. We must remember that Xenophon lived and wrote at a time when the Spartans exercised "hegemony over all of the Greeks." In the *Anabasis*, he maintains that their predominance was such that any Spartan "could do as he wished in the cities." Such power posed a singular danger to the safety of anyone they might consider a detractor of their rule. Indeed, as he spells out later in that book, to have opposed them openly

2. Ibid., 167.
3. *Anab.* 5.8.26.

would have been to play the part of a fool and to have harmed one's fatherland, friends, and family.[4] This external restraint on his freedom of expression goes a long way toward explaining Xenophon's allusive and elliptical style. While he gives us a satire on the shortcomings of the Spartans' domestic regime in the *Constitution of the Lacedaemonians* and extends that analysis in the *Hellenica* to consider the foreign policy toward which those defects lead, he then shows in the *Cyropaedia* how the attempt to overcome these difficulties by transforming an idealized Spartan republic into a full-fledged imperial power ultimately results in the "rebarbarization" of its citizens. Together, these writings serve as a warning against the political aspirations of his contemporaries.

If Xenophon is critical of imperial schemes and ambitions, he has little hope of preventing or curing them. "Having learned from Socrates that political life is not strictly speaking rational, Xenophon does not commit the error of acting as if it were."[5] Yet to hold that political life can never be altogether rational is not to assert that it is governed by forces that reason cannot grasp. The movement from republic to empire is driven in large part by the attempt to overcome certain defects or tensions within the republican regime itself. The tension between the republican principle of cultivating virtue in all and the practical necessity of discriminating among citizens on the oligarchic principle of wealth calls forth the effort to overcome the contradiction by unleashing the full economic potential of the peers' military might. Similarly, the tension between the republican claim to secure the common good through the strict rule of law and the manifest justice of rewarding individual merit inclines toward the establishment of an absolute monarch who will both embody the highest peak of political virtue and remedy the defects arising from the necessary generality of the law.[6] With greater clarity than perhaps any of his contemporaries, Xenophon both foresees the passing away of the polis and its distinctive way of life and explores the consequences of the almost inevitable emergence of empire on the Asiatic model.[7]

4. *Anab.* 6.1.26; 6.6.9, 12; 7.1.28–29; cf. *CL* 14.6 and *Hel.* 3.1.5.
5. Ruderman 1992, 132.
6. Cf. Aristotle *Politics* 1287a25–b36; 1292a33–b9; 1281a32–38; 1286a16–19.
7. Sinclair 1951, 287: "The *Cyropaedia* of Xenophon . . . has proved to be curiously prophetic of the fact that kingship, half Greek and half Oriental, dominated the eastern Mediterranean for the next three centuries after Alexander."

It would be strange if he were to fail to adapt his writings to his insight, especially as he had himself had such a powerful experience of the benefit to be derived from "the treasures that the wise men of old wrote down and left behind in their books."[8] He therefore mutes his criticisms of empire so as to increase the likelihood that his works will be preserved in the coming political order, while still providing some antidote against its worst excesses.[9] The wide circulation and popularity of the *Cyropaedia* in the Roman world testifies to both his prescience and rhetorical skills.

On a deeper level, however, Xenophon's reluctance to criticize Cyrus directly is dictated by his understanding of the shortcomings not just of empire but of political life in general. If Cyrus's empire fails to secure a common good that transcends defense against external enemies and the essentially private pleasures of the body, a common good that can reasonably or dependably call forth the kind of noble self-sacrifice it must always demand, the Persian republic suffers from related defects.

This becomes most apparent over the course of a conversation between Cyrus and his father that takes place on the eve of the departure of the Persian army for the war. This dialogue, which begins literally in the heart of Persia, on the threshold of the king's house, continues until they reach the distant border with Media, at the same time moving from a consideration of the core of republican morality to its periphery. Cambyses begins by declaring that the auspices are favorable and reminds Cyrus that he, too, has been taught the art of prophecy in order that he might always know the gods' counsels without depending on priests who might otherwise deceive or desert him (1.6.2). The topic of prophecy prompts Cyrus to recall other theological lessons he has heard from his father. To keep the gods well disposed and willing to give their advice, he should remember them in times of prosperity rather than calling on them only when in distress, just as one does with men. Cyrus appears to accept this view and, conscious of never having neglected them, is disposed to consider the gods as his friends (1.6.4; cf. 1.6.18, 46).

---

8. *Mem.* 1.6.14. For Xenophon's concern with future readers, see Dillery 1995, 161.

9. Consider, e.g., how Dio Chrysostom adopts material from the *Cyropaedia* to criticize the rule of Domitian (*Diogenes, or On Tyranny*).

A real difference of opinion emerges only when they turn to the subject of ruling.[10] According to Cambyses, for someone to provide for a household and to take care that he become himself really (δοχίμως) noble and good is a difficult and noble work for a man. But to know how to govern others so that they have all the necessities in abundance and are such as they ought to be, this is something to inspire wonder. Cyrus recalls hearing his father's views, yet now agrees only that "ruling nobly" is a very great work. In other words, he does not share Cambyses' opinion as to the difficulty or importance of becoming "truly good and noble" himself.[11] Or, rather, unlike Cambyses, Cyrus does not seem to admit the possibility that the virtues of the good man and those of the good ruler might differ. He is perhaps then not so much indifferent to becoming truly good and noble, as convinced that he already is or well on the way to becoming so. According to Cyrus, the good ruler ought to surpass the ruled "not in easy living but in taking forethought and loving to toil." And like an industrious shepherd rather than a hungry wolf, among the things he toils for is to provide those under him with the necessities of life in abundance so that they will all be as they should (1.6.8, 7). Cyrus appears then to share the conventional understanding of what makes a good ruler, as well as the conventional aspiration to be one. But the conventional understanding is not altogether unproblematic, as we can see from the extraordinary inferences Cyrus draws from it. He believes himself to possess the requisite qualities to such a degree that when he contemplates "ruling itself" and reflects on what he has seen of other men and their rulers, he concludes that it would be shameful to cower before them and not wish to go and fight. Cyrus knows firsthand, "beginning with our friends"—that is, the Medes—that some think a ruler should surpass his subjects in sumptuousness of fare, money, and longer hours of sleep, and, in general, enjoy greater luxury and ease. But because rule should go instead to those with the appropriate virtues, and as Cyrus believes himself to possess these more than do others, there is no reason in principle why he should not take their places. Here,

10. Cyrus's opinions about the gods rest on his father's word; but he has other evidence to consult when it comes to "ruling itself." Compare ἀκούσας σου at 1.6.3 and its repetition at 1.6.6, with σκοπῶν λογίζωμαι and ἰδὼν κατανοήσω at 1.6.8.

11. Bruell 1987, 102. Cf. *CL* 15.5 for the importance Xenophon placed on the distinction between ruling and being worthy to rule.

then, for the first time, the almost limitless nature of Cyrus's ambition stands revealed before his father; and its roots would seem to lie in the respectable opinion that rulers should be superior to the ruled in virtue. The apparently wholesome exhortation to make oneself eminently qualified to rule opens a potentially limitless prospect. Now normally one would expect a claim to rule based on superior foresight, love of toil, and endurance in the face of hardship to be balanced or limited by other virtues. Justice, for instance, to say nothing of a concern with nobility (cf. 1.5.13), would seem to dictate that Cyrus help his relations and allies, rather than fight with and overthrow them, especially because it was for the former task that the Council made him general (1.5.4–5). And in Persia justice is understood to include obedience to the laws, not to mention respect for elders. Yet we have seen that Cyrus has been inclined from an early age not to take this claim too much to heart, and his time at Astyages' court exposes him to other alternatives. His multicultural education appears then to have helped pave the way for the inclusion of their Median "friends" among those whom he thinks himself worthy to rule and thus conquer. What is more surprising, though, is that this proposal does not meet with anything like the kind of outrage or moral indignation that one might expect on the part of Cambyses. This is all the more striking given that Cyrus's understanding of what constitutes the highest claim to rule leaves no room for recognition of the authority of the Council that elected him general, and, when carried to its logical conclusion, poses as great a threat to Cambyses as to Cyaxares. But Cyrus has chosen this moment of candor with his usual exquisite timing. He, not his father, now stands at the head of the Persian army. If, as Cambyses himself admits, arguments made by someone who is in control of a well-ordered military force are for that very reason often more persuasive (1.6.11), those made by the unarmed must be correspondingly weaker, regardless of their "merits." To receive an attentive hearing, someone arguing from a position of weakness must adapt his speech to the interests and passions of the powerful. If Cambyses is to defend himself and the integrity of the Persian regime from the imperial ambitions of his son, he must do so in a manner calculated to appeal to those ambitions. This approach also serves to establish his credentials as a hard-nosed, and therefore valuable, advisor.

Cambyses begins by pointing out that to be ranged against contemptible opponents is not always enough to guarantee victory:

"But son," he said, "there are some respects in which one must contend not against human beings but against matters themselves (πρὸς αὐτὰ τὰ πράγματα), and it is not very easy to surpass them readily. You doubtless know that if the army does not have the necessary provisions, your rule will dissolve at once."

"But father," he said, "Cyaxares says that he will provide these things for all who come from here, no matter how many they may be."

"So, son," he said, "you are going off trusting in the funds of Cyaxares?"

"I am," said Cyrus.

"Well," said he, "do you know how much he has?"

"No, by Zeus," said Cyrus, "I don't."

"And you nevertheless trust in these uncertainties? Don't you know that you will need many things and that now he must of necessity spend for many other things?"

"I know," said Cyrus.

"But if his expenses outstrip him, or he is willing to lie to you, what will the condition of your army be then?" (1.6.9)

Cyrus, who has perhaps relied on an outdated assessment of his opponent's capacities, has not considered that the uncle whom he is planning to supplant might anticipate his intent (cf. 1.4.9) and have something similar in mind for him. Sobered by this oversight and encouraged by his father's lack of moral pretense or outrage, Cyrus drops what little remains of his own posturing and asks forthrightly for advice "while we are still in friendly territory," that is, before they cross over into the territory of their "allies," the Medes (1.6.9).

The fact that Cyrus now heads the Persian army is not the only difficulty Cambyses must overcome in his effort to moderate his son's ambition to conquer. An even greater obstacle or complication arises from the circumstances that have contributed to placing Cyrus there. The expansion of the Assyrian empire does pose a genuine threat to the very existence of the Persian republic. Cyrus's military genius and other skills, along with his indomitable spirit to emerge victorious from every contest, make him a valuable resource, perhaps one indispensable for the country's defense. But these qualities combine in such a way as to make him both the greatest hope and the greatest threat to the survival of the regime. Inasmuch as Cyrus is the defender of

Persia against an aggressive imperial power, Cambyses must share with him his experience and knowledge of how best to defeat it. But as Cyrus also seems willing to pursue victory at the possible expense of Persia, he must do his best to moderate that desire. The need to maintain this delicate balance governs Cambyses' speech throughout this conversation and limits what he can say and do himself: for example, if he points out the difficulty of getting supplies for the army and keeping the soldiers healthy, he must also make clear the best means to do so (1.6.9–10, 15–16). Thus Cambyses' advice stands in tension with itself, and necessarily so, certain parts actually undermining others. The deepest source of this tension comes to light most clearly in their discussion of the best way to obtain the obedience and love of one's soldiers.

In order to keep the soldiers in line, Cyrus intends to follow the example of his father, his teachers, and the laws. They all praise and honor the obedient, while dishonoring and punishing the disobedient. Cambyses agrees (and in doing so renders his judgment on the true nature of Persian education) that this is indeed the way to obtain "obedience by compulsion" (τὸ ἀνάγκῃ ἕπεσθαι). But Cyrus ignores, or perhaps has no experience with, a better and shorter road, the one that leads to "willing obedience" (τὸ ἑκόντας πείθεσθαι, 1.6.21; cf. *Mem.* 2.1.29). This kind of obedience men render with great pleasure to those whom they think more prudent about their own interests than they are themselves. Its power is manifest in the eagerness with which the sick follow a doctor's orders and passengers at sea the directions of the pilot. Travelers, too, assiduously stick with those whom they believe to be more familiar with the roads. But if human beings think that they will incur some harm by doing so, punishments and rewards cannot make them willing to obey. "For no one willingly accepts even a gift when it brings him harm" (1.6.20–21).[12]

Cyrus immediately understands his father to mean that what is most effective in keeping subjects obedient is then "*to seem to be more prudent than they*" (1.6.22; emphasis added). If the best or strongest kind of obedience depends upon the will, and the will depends upon the mind or the opinions that guide it, a ruler must

---

12. Cf. *Mem.* 3.9.4, *Hel.* 2.3.33 and 7.1.5 for other expressions of this fundamental thesis.

be attentive to the impression he makes there. Accordingly, Cyrus asks his father how he might gain a "reputation" as quickly as possible, for without it whatever prudence he does possess will remain to some extent politically ineffective.[13] But if Cyrus hopes in this way to remain satisfied with the mere appearance of prudence and to avoid the long and difficult task of actually becoming prudent, Cambyses is ready with a fatherly rebuke:

If you wish to seem to be a good farmer when you are not—or horseman, doctor, flute player, or anything whatsoever—consider how many things you must contrive for the sake of so seeming. Even if you should persuade many to praise you in order to get a good reputation, and procure fine equipment for each of these [arts], you would deceive only for the moment, or a little bit beyond. And when put to the test, you would be refuted and exposed as a boaster. (1.6.22)

To gain a secure reputation for prudence, one must become prudent in reality through an assiduous devotion to learning the necessary arts, much as Cyrus has already done with regard to tactics. But political and military success frequently depend upon foresight about particulars, whereas the arts can predict and control only the outcome of events in general.[14] Cyrus must recognize the limits of prudence and concerning "those things that can neither be learned nor foreseen by human foresight" make inquiries of the gods "through prophecy." True human prudence includes, then, an awareness of its own limitations, and this awareness inclines toward a certain dependence upon the gods. But as the gods might sometimes wish to do harm, something that Cambyses is now willing to admit (1.6.18; cf. 1.6.4, 46), it is best to avoid exposing oneself to dangerous or risky situations whenever possible. Prudence, at least in politics, seems indistinguishable from a cautious and conservative regard for self-preservation (cf. 3.1.20, 24–25).

The superiority of willing obedience to obedience by compulsion, the inevitable detection and punishment of boasters, the need for genuine yet hard-to-acquire prudence, the limitations of that prudence, the connection of political success to the disposition of the gods, and

13. Plato *Republic* 488d–89a.
14. *Mem.* 1.1.6–9.

the doubt that their disposition will always be favorable: all of these arguments Cambyses tailors to dampen Cyrus's ambitions by making him less confident of their attainment. Yet there are certain difficulties with Cambyses' advice and admonitions. For his part, Cyrus does not acknowledge their soundness as he did with his father's earlier suggestions.[15] Willing obedience may be preferable and stronger than obedience by compulsion, but it is not always possible or even necessary to obtain it. Human beings defer to prudence when they believe this to be in their best interest. Yet even the most prudent ruler, and especially a general at war, must sometimes ask, indeed require, the sacrifice of individual interests. To obtain obedience at such times, some form of compulsion, open or otherwise, remains a necessity. For no one willingly accepts even a gift if he believes that to do so is to his disadvantage. Whatever else its merits, willing obedience can never entirely replace obedience by compulsion, at least not so long as war or law remain essential elements of political life.

Cyrus therefore responds to his father's emphasis on prudence and the kind of obedience it supposedly gives rise to, not with approval, but by declaring that "being loved by one's subjects" is among "the greatest matters." He intends to rely on this other, potentially greater motivation to supplement what he takes to be the compulsions of punishments and praise (cf. 5.1.12; 7.5.60); and he plans to obtain their love by "being manifest in doing good for them" (1.6.24). Cambyses is quick to point out that "it is difficult to be able at all times to do good for those for whom one would like to do good." But even he must admit that a ruler can secure the love of his subjects merely if "he shows himself" to rejoice in their prosperity and to commiserate in their misfortunes, and if he "appears" eager to help them and fearful lest they suffer any harm. Soldiers in particular are won over when their ruler "shows himself" to seek out a bigger share of their common hardships by enduring more heat, cold, and toil than all the rest. Cambyses' stress on the utility of appearances implies that a ruler need not always do or be these things in reality. He even gives some further encouragement to Cyrus with the observation that these common burdens do not in fact weigh equally on a ruler, for to him belongs the greatest honor of the undertaking, and, conscious that nothing he

15. Cf. 1.6.24 with 1.6.19, 16, 11, 9.

does goes unobserved, his labors in fact become "somewhat lighter" (1.6.25; cf. 8.2.22). Despite appearances, Cyrus will then endure less, not more, of the army's hardships. But this means that the soldiers' love for him will be based at least in part on an illusion. The ability to exploit this mistaken impression, to say nothing of the utility of inspiring his followers from time to time with great but false hopes (1.6.19; cf. *Mem.* 4.2.17), ameliorates the difficulty of not always being able to benefit those whom he would wish. But if this deception, which amounts to a kind of boasting, is a useful tool to gain his men's love, why could it not be equally useful in obtaining their willing obedience, for example, by persuading them that their best interests are being pursued even when they are not? "By nature all believe that they love those by whom they believe they are benefited"(*Oec.* 20.29). Moreover, Cambyses' dire warning about the consequences of practicing false prudence and boasting, an argument that boils down to the utilitarian nostrum that honesty is the best policy, is only to be feared if the deception fails to reduce its victims to a state in which they have no effective means to protest.[16] Even granting the dubious assertion that all such falsehoods must eventually come to light, "the little bit" of time between their implementation and discovery may well suffice for the achievement of some important plan (cf. 3.3.51; 4.5.16, with 8.5.22–27). Cyaxares quickly discovers the deceit behind his nephew's request to borrow cavalry, but nevertheless finds himself completely undone (4.4.9; 5.5.32–36). If society remains essentially and irremediably constituted by opinion, then the "effectual truth" of politics is "appearances," and deceit the key to mastery.

Cambyses' argument against relying on deception, which issues in a rejoinder to depend instead upon the counsels of the gods, is therefore itself deceitful and intentionally so. Inasmuch as he knows, or strongly suspects, that Cyrus's desire for limitless conquests conflicts with the best interests of the republican regime, he seeks to moderate that desire by denying the utility of deception and by overstating the importance of genuine prudence or knowledge as the necessary means to political success. As the lesser of two powers, he has almost no choice but to employ falsehoods himself in his effort to correct or curb his son. Cyrus is not taken in, however, and immediately shifts the discussion

16. Consider 3.3.51–52 with *CL* 9.1.

to a topic where his father is forced to concede the utility of deception. According to his own statement, we would expect Cambyses to pay a price for having his ruse so soon discovered. And he does. At the conclusion of the discussion of how to win the love of his men, Cyrus professes the opinion that for a well-prepared general, "moderation" consists in "desiring to fight against the enemy as quickly as possible." Cambyses can only respond by trying to insert at least one qualification: Cyrus should attack only if he is sure to gain some advantage from it (πλεῖον ἕξειν, 1.6.26).[17] The cool calculation of "enlightened" self-interest is the final barrier he places in the path of his son's ambition. But to make this argument, he is forced to invoke the principle said to be most characteristic of tyranny (1.3.18). Impelled by the force of Cyrus's questioning, the ensuing discussion of "how most of all to take advantage of enemies" lays bare the questionable foundation of the peers' friendship for one another, and, with it, the Persian regime's claim to care especially for the common good (1.2.3).

Cambyses maintains that to take advantage of the enemy is neither an easy nor a simple task (ἁπλοῦν, literally "single"). To do so, one must be a plotter and a dissembler, treacherous and deceiving, a thief and a robber, and ready to take advantage of one's enemies in all things.[18] Cyrus seems genuinely surprised, if not by the content, then at least by the candor and boldness of this revelation. "O Heracles, father, what sort of man do you say I must become?" he asks with a laugh.[19] Cambyses responds that precisely this sort of man is "both most just and most lawful" (1.6.27). Cyrus is puzzled. If such behavior is the peak of justice, why as boys were they taught just the opposite? Cambyses defends the teachers' practice by emphasizing the distinction between friends and enemies. Toward their fellow citizens, they should still abide by the rules given them in childhood. Taking advantage is to be practiced only against their enemies. As for the actual instruction in how to harm them, this was not neglected, but taught to the children covertly. Just as they learned to shoot by aiming at a mark instead of at one another, so they learned to take advantage in war by fighting

17. Cf. *Hipparchicus* 4.13.
18. Cf. 6.3.15, *Mem.* 3.1.6–7; Machiavelli, *Prince*, ch. 15.
19. On the whole, Persian life is characterized more by tears than laughter. Cf. 2.2.14, 2.3.1.

on unequal terms against the animals that they hunted with nets, snares, and pits. In this way, the boys learn the skills necessary to harm enemies, should this ever be required, while avoiding any injury to their fellows. What seems to make this double teaching necessary is the fact that men are divided into potentially hostile cities and tribes. Were there only one peaceful, universal nation, lawful conduct would perhaps admit of no exceptions.[20] Justice would again be something simple.[21] However, in the present, imperfect world, the constant threat of war demands two different standards of justice, one for friends, another for enemies.[22]

This response leaves Cyrus perplexed, and rightly so, for it fails to address his original objection. Even if it is necessary to distinguish between the treatment of friends and enemies, why was this not explained to the children in the beginning? Moreover, the actual practice of the teachers as it now stands revealed serves to undermine the distinction. For to teach the necessary skills of war, they themselves practiced a kind of covert deception on the children, even if only to prevent them from harming one another. Thus the original commandment not to deceive, which the need to prepare for war requires be qualified by the distinction between friends and enemies, seems to demand yet another qualification: sometimes it is apparently permitted to deceive even friends (cf. 6.1.39ff., 7.5.46). Or were these teachers not the children's friends? Cyrus immediately sees the inadequacy of the simple distinction between friends and enemies, and, dropping it altogether, insists that "because it is useful to know how to benefit and how to harm human beings, both these things should have been taught with human beings as well" (1.6.30).[23] Cyrus's intransigent pursuit of what is useful prompts Cambyses to tell a story about a former teacher, an almost Socratic figure, who once taught justice in the very way Cyrus now bids:

But it is said, son, that in the time of our ancestors there was once a man, a teacher of the boys, who taught the boys justice in the way you insist, both to

20. Cf. *Hipparchicus* 5.9.
21. See 3.1.32 for another instance in which justice becomes something "single/simple."
22. Cf. *Mem.* 4.2.12–18.
23. An alternative manuscript reading is "against human beings."

lie and not to lie, to deceive and not to deceive, to slander and not to slander, to take advantage and not to take advantage. He defined which of these one must do to friends and which to enemies. And he taught moreover that it was just to deceive even one's friends, at least for a good [end], and to steal the things of friends for a good [end] (ἐπὶ ἀγαθῷ). (1.6.31)[24]

Now to teach these things properly, it was of course necessary to have the boys practice on one another. But "being naturally suited to deceive well and take advantage well, and perhaps also being not unnaturally lovers of gain, [some] did not refrain from trying to take advantage even of their friends" (1.6.31–32). As a consequence of the ensuing disorder, there came to be the rule, still in use among them, that children be taught (like house slaves) "simply" to tell the truth, not to deceive, and not to take advantage. Those who disobey are punished and hence inured by habit to become tamer citizens. Only when they are about the age of Cyrus is it considered safe to reveal what is lawful toward enemies, for if they have grown up together in mutual respect, they do not seem to break away and become savage when presented with this supplementary teaching (1.6.33–34).

Whether historically true or not, Cambyses' story does have the merit of addressing Cyrus's original concern about the children's apparently defective education, although it raises as many questions as it resolves. Now, it appears, not so much the possibility of war but rather the elusive and shifting character of any particular or contingent good lies at the root of the inadequacy of any single or simple teaching about justice, such as obedience to law, as is taught in the Persian schools.[25] The exceptional stresses of war merely bring to the surface deficiencies already present in the established laws, although perhaps less pressing in times of peace. If this former teacher's desire to attempt such an experiment in the first place casts doubt on the ultimate respectability of the laws, and therefore on justice understood as obedience to law, its failure reveals not so much the solidity or goodness of those laws but the hollowness of the peers' friendship for one another (and, by implication, their hostility to foreigners as such), a friendship that rests at bottom on habits inculcated by force and reinforced with shame. This, and not some shared common good, is what ultimately binds

24. Cf. *Mem.* 3.1.6, 4.2.11–20; Plato *Republic* 331c, 333a–334b.
25. Cf. *Mem.* 4.2.17, 3.8.1–3, 4.6.8.

them together. Of course, one could point out that the peers do share a common good or interest in providing for their mutual defense and keeping down the commoners. Yet, inasmuch as it is founded on a calculation of self-interest, like the justice of a band of thieves, it carries no permanent sense of duty or obligation.[26] Indeed, it is the kind of benefit that cannot bear the open avowal of its true nature.[27]

What is the proper response to the insights gained from this new or supplementary teaching about justice? The reaction hoped for by the teachers, and upon which the republican regime depends, is that the young man accepts the necessity of taking advantage of enemies by whatever means but remains bound by the law in his relations with fellow citizens. Should it occur to him that his earlier education was based on a mixture of compulsion and deceit, this only serves to deepen his sense of loyalty. The laws, like a loving but firm parent, administer all this for his own good. A citizen might, and even should, feel gratitude for the beatings and tears inflicted in his youth. Such is the response of Aglaitadas, the sole Persian to defend their ancestral ways over and against the innovations introduced by Cyrus. But as this loyal peer's opposition suggests, Cyrus is himself unlikely to have responded in this way. Indeed, for such a revelation to evoke a loyal response, it seems necessary for citizens to have been reared together as boys (συντεθραμμένοι, 1.6.34; cf. 2.1.28). But Cyrus did most of his growing up (ἐτρέφετο) on his own, far away in Media (1.4.1).

It seems more plausible that when properly understood, debunking the Persian claim to devote themselves especially to virtue and the common good produces in the soul a certain dissatisfaction with the regime. And this dissatisfaction itself may give rise to the ambition to found a new kind of political community. If full Persian citizenship depends more on birth than intrinsic merit (1.2.15), and the peers' friendship for one another rests on a false foundation, why not work to establish a regime where arbitrary distinctions between friends and enemies no longer dominate political life, a regime cosmopolitan in character and tending toward a world-state ordered for the sake of true human virtue, rather than one where virtue is subordinated to, and

---

26. Cf. Plato *Republic* 352b c.

27. Cyrus voices his most candid assessment of the Persian regime in a private conversation with a foreigner (2.1.3).

even constituted by, the demands of a parochial society? Proceeding from his denunciations of the injustice inherent in narrow republican patriotism, Cyrus frequently looks to the creation of a worldwide meritocracy in which the duties of citizenship and humanity will be reconciled (e.g., 2.2.26). Yet the foreseeable limitations that govern Cyrus's construction of an empire make it anything but this hoped for utopia. It turns out to be at least as corrupt as republican Persia, and, in addition, much more unstable (7.5; 8.8).

The experiment in teaching the Persian children how to be bad for a good end makes them experts in deception, in effect releasing them from the constraints of law. The disastrous results would clearly seem to indicate that nothing but habit and fear of punishment stand in the way of our helping an enemy, or harming a friend, should this satisfy our natural love of gain. Not so much any condition of natural scarcity, but rather this passion of unlimited scope (8.2.20–22), lies at the heart of conflicts not only between nations and civil factions but between individuals as well.[28] The perpetual war of every one against every one that it creates makes any lasting or more than mercenary friendship impossible or foolish. Enemies are infinitely numerous, and one's only true and constant "friend" is oneself. Attachment to Persia, a regime that admittedly treats its citizens like domestic slaves for much, if not all, of their lives,[29] becomes not a question of loyalty or duty, but a mere calculation of its value as a means or tool to essentially individual, if not altogether private, ends.

Does this then mean that the empty pretensions of the republican claim to secure a genuine common good and the impossibility of establishing a just and universal empire attest to the wisdom of seeking political power for the sake of self-aggrandizement, no matter what the cost to others, an understanding of politics that finds its popular expression in the widespread admiration for successful tyrants (1.1.1)? Such a reading of the *Cyropaedia* would confirm the accusation leveled against Xenophon by Machiavelli, namely, that this book covertly instructs its more astute readers (Caesars, not Scipios) in how to pursue their ambitions even, or especially, at the expense of republican government—an instruction less beneficent in both intention and

28. *Hiero* 4.6; *Mem.* 2.6.21.
29. Consider in this light ἐλευθέρα ἀγορὰ καλουμένη at 1.2.3. Cf. 1.1.2.

effect than his own more public and "Manlian" airing of similar facts.[30] This conclusion would follow were there not another and possibly more coherent response to these revelations about the true nature of political life, both republican and imperial, a response embodied in the character of Cambyses. The insight that the Persian education in justice is in fact an indoctrination in the service of collective selfishness, an awareness facilitated in Cyrus's case by his exposure at a tender age to another, if equally defective, understanding of justice in Media, is nevertheless a genuine liberation and one shared by Cambyses, to say nothing of our author. Yet in the case of Cyrus it appears to be only a partial or incomplete liberation, insofar as he remains strongly attached to what is common to the Persian and Median view, namely, a belief in the nobility and goodness of "ruling itself" (1.6.7–9; cf. 1.6.27). Cyrus may dismiss the kind of justice born from the dictates of political society; he may act without serious regard for conventional restraints; yet at no point does he ever question the understanding of nobility that political society exalts. He still pursues the traditional goal of political rule and the honor it brings.

Cambyses and Xenophon harbor no illusions about the character of the Persian regime. Neither expresses anything like the passionate indignation that moves republican partisans such as Mandane and Aglaitadas. And having thought through the nature of the conventional limitations imposed and bred by habit, they are as little bound by them as Cyrus. Yet Cambyses remains somehow loyal to Persia and on behalf of the city, tries to check his son's dangerous ambitions. One might take this loyalty to derive from his position as king. In defending republican Persia, he simply defends himself and his own exalted position. But this attachment, to say nothing of his moderation and equanimity, derives precisely from his unorthodox view of the desirability of political rule. Cambyses shares Cyrus's awareness of the shortcomings of political justice, but in his greater seriousness about justice, he radicalizes this insight to call into question the status of the political understanding of nobility as well. This leads him, unlike Cyrus, to distinguish between becoming noble and good himself and ruling, and to prefer the former to the latter whenever possible (1.6.7).[31] In other words, he does not

30. Machiavelli, *Discourses*, 3.22; *Prince*, chs. 17 and 18.
31. Bruell 1987, 102.

understand the obstacles, perhaps even necessities, that stand in the way of ordering society for the sake of virtue to imply the impossibility or foolishness of pursuing virtue altogether.[32] True virtue and nobility might still exist, although in part at a transpolitical level. But if this is so, one must wonder why Cambyses does not make more of an effort to correct his son's mistaken impression of the nobility of political rule (1.6.9). Perhaps Cyrus's too early and too easy deprecation of the claims of political justice prevents him from ever pursuing the full implications of that devaluation (1.3.17–18).[33] Or perhaps, given the circumstances, Cambyses judges that the discouragement likely to follow in the immediate wake of such a correction poses a greater threat to Cyrus's ability to fulfill his duties as general than his passion for imperial rule does to the integrity of the republican regime. Instead, he turns to the gods. Cambyses begins their conversation with a favorable if unorthodox reading of the signs, one intended both to inspire confidence in the undertaking and to put Cyrus on guard against those who would try to manipulate or falsify the auspices (1.6.12). After discovering his son's ultimate intentions, he concludes by declaring the fickle and unfathomable will of the gods to be the best grounds for caution and contentment with one's lot (1.6.46).[34] When they arrive at the border of Persia, they pray, embrace, and then part. Cambyses returns to "the city,"[35] even in the face of its misleading claims to respectability. Cyrus continues on to empire. The father's failure to moderate his son's political ambition illustrates certain limits to the power of rational discourse.[36]

The *Cyropaedia* presents a comparison of the relative strengths and weaknesses of republican and imperial politics. But it also demonstrates the contradictions and necessities that limit the attainment of justice and the common good in either regime. In other words, if Xenophon's Persia represents classical republicanism at its best and Cyrus's Persian empire the failed attempt to overcome its defects, then the *Cyropaedia* as a whole constitutes a critique of political life in the classical world *tout court*. Certainly Xenophon's description of the

32. Cf. Machiavelli, *Prince*, ch 15.
33. Cf 1.6.35; Plato *Republic* 409b; *Sophist* 251b–c.
34. Cf. *Hel.* 4.3.14.
35. Reading πόλιν at 2.1.1 with MS z.
36. Cf. *Mem.* 1.2.12–18; Plato *Republic* 548e–549d.

short-lived and hollow splendor of the empire and the particularly dire consequences of its collapse is meant to provide a defense of the stable if austere politics of the republican regime.[37] But it is the kind of quiet or backhand defense that the regime itself would find intolerable. Still, the corruption of the republic and the instability and collapse of the empire do provide a genuine education in the necessities governing political life; they are, at least potentially, not without some good effect. Xenophon may tempt us with the charms of an austere and virtuous republic devoted to producing good men, or with the portrait of a perfect prince capable of governing the entire world; he may engage our deepest passions for justice, glory, and unlimited wealth; but he then purges them by demonstrating the impossibility, and even the undesirability, of their full realization. In short, he adopts the rhetorical strategy of Cambyses, who suggests that sometimes men inspired by great hopes can be benefited by being led to something less than their complete fulfillment (1.6.19).[38] By showing the necessities that limit the attainment of justice in all regimes, Xenophon prevents us from giving ourselves wholeheartedly to any one, or to political life altogether. Such is the subtle pedagogy of the *Cyropaedia*.

This means that the education that Xenophon intends for his reader differs significantly from the one that Cyrus receives, and that the latter is essentially defective. But if education is man's greatest good, as Xenophon's Socrates declares it to be,[39] and Cyrus ultimately lacks a true one, we would expect this defect to become manifest in some way. Certain characters in the *Cyropaedia* do genuinely admire Cyrus; they even declare him beautiful and wise.[40] But Tigranes, Xenophon's alter ego in the book, remains silent in the midst of his comrades' general acclamation of their leader (5.1.27; cf. 3.1.41). Indicating his judgment of their relative worth, Xenophon himself certainly never says of Cyrus what he professes to believe of Socrates: "He seemed to me himself blessedly happy (μακάριος) and to lead those who listened to him to gentlemanliness."[41] One might infer from this comparison that what Xenophon most condemns is Cyrus's willingness to pursue

37. Bruell 1987, 101.
38. Cf. *Mem.* 3.5, 3.6.
39. *Apol.* 21.
40. 3.1.41, 3.3.4, 5.1.24–26, 28–29; cf. *Hel.* 7.1.12.
41. *Mem.* 1.6.14; cf. 4.8.11.

his own interests at the expense or corruption of the nobility of others. And it is regrettable that the Persians lose their freedom and equality to his supremacy. Yet our sympathies are muted by recalling that they merely suffer a fate that they themselves hoped to inflict upon the rest of the world. Cyrus may take advantage of them, but he does so largely through their own willingness to take advantage of others. From Xenophon's perspective, it is hard to wax indignant at his greater competence. It would be more accurate to conclude that Cyrus's exercise of his uncanny ability to get the better of others, to do as he likes in almost any situation,[42] stands in the way of the realization and pursuit of his true interest, whether or not this goes undetected or unpunished by others.[43] In this way Xenophon's portrait of a perfect prince brings home to us how much is at stake in the possibility of a genuine education.

42. Cf. *Mem.* 1.2.14.
43. Cf. 1.6.45–46; Machiavelli, *Discourses*, 3.23.6.

Works Cited

Alberti, Leon Battista. [1404–72].

    1960–73.   *Opere volgari*. Edited by Cecil Grayson, 3 vols. Crittori d'Italia, no. 218, Bari: G. Laterza.

Anderson, J. K.

    1974.   *Xenophon*. New York: Scribner.

Bartlett, Robert.

    1996.   "Xenophon's *Symposium*." In *Xenophon's Shorter Socratic Writings*, edited by Robert Bartlett. Ithaca, N.Y.: Cornell University Press.

Bizos, Marcel.

    1971–73.   *Cyropédie, I–II*. Paris: Les Belles Lettres.

Bolingbroke, Henry St. John, 1st viscount.

    1752.   *Letters on the Study and Use of History*. London: A. Millar.

Bornemann, Friedrich.

    1819.   *Die Epilog der Cyropaedie von Xenophon*. Leipzig: Hinrichs.

Bruell, Christopher.

    1969.   "Xenophon's *Education of Cyrus*." Ph.D. diss., University of Chicago.

    ———.

    1987.   "Xenophon." In *History of Political Philosophy*, edited by Leo Strauss and Joseph Cropsey. Chicago: University of Chicago Press.

    ———.

    1988.   "Xenophon and His Socrates." *Interpretation* (16), 295–306.

Carlier, Pierre.

    1978.   "L'idée de monarchie impériale dans *La Cyropédie*." *Ktema* 3: 133–63.

Cartledge, Paul.

    1987.   *Agesilaos and the Crisis of Sparta*. Baltimore: Johns Hopkins University Press.

Castiglione, Baldassare [1518].
    1968.   *Il cortegiano*. Edited by Ghino Ghinassi. Florence: Sansoni.
Cobet, C. G.
    1875.   "De Xenophontis Cyrupaediae epilogo." *Mnemosyne* 3: 66–72.
Croiset, Alfred.
    1873.   *Xénophon: son caractère et son talent*. Toulouse: Thorin.
Dadachanjee, R. K.
    1904.   "On the *Cyropaedia*." *Journal of the Bombay Branch of the
                 Royal Asiatic Society* 21: 552–61.
Delebecque, Edouard.
    1957.   *Essai sur la vie de Xénophon*. Paris: C. Klincksieck.
⸻.
    1978.   *Cyropédie III*. Paris: Les Belles Lettres.
Diels, Hermann.
    1903.   *Die fragmente der Vorsokratiker*. Berlin: Weidemann.
Dillery, John.
    1995.   *Xenophon and the History of His Times*. London: Routledge.
Due, Bodil.
    1989.   *The* Cyropaedia: *Xenophon's Aims and Methods*. Aarhus:
                 Aarhus University Press.
Eichler, Gustav.
    1880.   *De Cyrupaediae capite extremo*. Leipzig: Grimmae.
Farber, Joel.
    1979.   "The *Cyropaedia* and Hellenic Kingship." *American Journal
                 of Philology* 100: 497–514.
Ferrari, Franco.
    1995.   *Ciropedia*. Milan: Rizzoli.
Ferrari, G. R. F.
    1997.   "Strauss' Plato." *Arion* (Fall): 36–65.
Forde, Steven.
    1989.   *The Ambition to Rule: Alcibiades and the Politics of Imperi-
                 alism in Thucydides*. Ithaca, N.Y.: Cornell University Press.
Garin, Eugenio.
    1972.   *Portraits from the Quattrocento*. Translated by Victor and
                 Elizabeth Velen. New York: Harper & Row.
Gautier, Léopold.
    1911.   *La Langue de Xénophon*. Geneva: n.p.
Georges, Pericles.
    1994.   *Barbarian Asia and the Greek Experience*. Baltimore: Johns
                 Hopkins University Press.
Gera, Deborah Levine.
    1993.   *Xenophon's* Cyropaedia: *Style, Genre, and Literary Technique*.
                 Oxford: Clarendon Press.

Giannantoni, Gabriele.
1985.   *Socraticorum reliquiare*. Naples: Edizioni dell'Ateneo.
Gibbon, Edward [1776–88].
1994.   *The History of the Decline and Fall of the Roman Empire*, 3
          vols. London: Penguin Classics.
Grant, Alexander.
1871.   *Xenophon*. Philadelphia: Lippincott.
Gray, Vivienne.
1986.   "Xenophon's *Hiero* and the Meeting of the Wise Man and
          Tyrant in Greek Literature." *Classics Quarterly* 36: 115–23.

———.

1989.   *The Character of Xenophon's Hellenica*. Baltimore: Johns
          Hopkins University Press.
Higgins, William Edward.
1977.   *Xenophon the Athenian: The Problem of the Individual and
          the Society of the Polis*. Albany: State University of New York
          Press.
Hirsch, Steven W.
1985.   *The Friendship of the Barbarians: Xenophon and the Persian
          Empire*. Hanover, N.H.: University Press of New England.
Hunt, Peter.
1998.   *Slaves, Warfare, and Ideology in the Greek Historians*. Cam-
          bridge: Cambridge University Press.
Keller, W. J.
1911.   "Xenophon's Acquaintance with the History of Herodotus."
          Classical Journal 6: 252–59, 347.
Linke, Karl.
1874.   *De Xenophonteo Cyropaediae interpolationibus*. Berlin.
Luccioni, Jean.
1949.   *Les idées politiques et sociales de Xénophon*. Paris: Ophrys.

———.

1953.   *Xénophon et le socratisme*. Paris: Presses universitaires de
          France.
Macfarland, Joseph.
1999.   "Machiavelli's Imagination of Excellent Men: An Appraisal of
          the Lives of Cosimo de'Medici and Castruccio Castracani."
          American Political Science Review 93: 133–46.
Machiavelli, Niccolò [1469–1527].
1985.   *The Prince*. Translated by Harvey C. Mansfield. Chicago:
          University of Chicago Press.

———.

1988.   *Opere*. Edited by Ezio Raimondi. Milan: Mursia.

————.

   1996.   *Discourses on Livy*. Translated by Harvey C. Mansfield and
             Nathan Tarcov. Chicago: University of Chicago Press.

Miller, Walter.

   1983.   *Cyropaedia: Text and Translation*. Cambridge, Mass.: Harvard
             University Press.

Milton, John.

   1958.   *Prose Writings*. London: Dent.

Momigliano, Arnaldo.

   1966.   "Per l'unità logica della ΛΑΚΕΔΑΙΜΟΝΙΩΝ ΠΟΛΙΤΕΙΑ di
             Senofonte." In *Terzo contributo alla storia degli studi classici
             e del mondo antico*. Rome: Edizioni de storia e letteratura.

————.

   1967.   "Ermeneutica e pensiero politico classico in Leo Strauss."
             Rivista storica italiana 79: 1164–72.

————.

   1991.   *The Development of Greek Biography*. Cambridge, Mass.:
             Harvard University Press.

Montaigne, Michel [1533–92].

   1950.   *Essais*. Paris: Gallimard.

Morrison, Donald.

   1987.   "On Professor Vlastos' Xenophon." *Ancient Philosophy* 7: 9–
             22.

————.

   1988.   *Bibliography of Editions, Translations, and Commentary on
             Xenophon's Socratic Writings: 1600–Present*. Pittsburgh:
             Mathesis Publications.

————.

   1995.   "Xenophon's Socrates on the Just and the Lawful." *Ancient
             Philosophy* 15: 329–477.

Mueller-Goldingen, Christian.

   1995.   *Untersuchungen zu Xenophons Kyrupädie*. Stuttgart: Teub-
             ner.

Munscher, Karl.

   1920.   "Xenophon in der griechisch-romischen Literatur." *Philologus*
             13.

Mure, William.

   1857.   *A Critical History of the Language and Literature of Ancient
             Greece*. London: Longman.

Newell, Waller Randy.

   1981.   "Xenophon's *Education of Cyrus* and the Classical Critique of
             Liberalism." Ph.D. diss., Yale University, 1981.

Niebuhr, Bathold Georg.
   1828.   *Kleine historische und philosophische Schriften*, Vol. 1. Bonn: E. Weber.
Orwin, Clifford.
   1994.   *The Humanity of Thucydides*. Princeton, N.J.: Princeton University Press.
Pangle, Thomas.
   1994.   "Socrates in the Context of Xenophon's Political Writings." In *The Socratic Movement*, edited by Paul Vander Waerdt. Ithaca, N.Y.: Cornell University Press.
Platina, Bartolomeo Sacchi [1421–81].
   1979.   *De Principe*. Edited by Giacomo Ferrau. Palermo: Il Vespro.
Pomeroy, Sarah.
   1994.   *Xenophon Oeconomicus: A Social and Historical Commentary*. Oxford: Clarendon Press.

   ———.
   1996.   Review of *Xenophon's Shorter Socratic Writings*, edited by Robert Bartlett. *Bryn Mawr Classical Review*, September.
Pontano, Giovanni [1426–1503].
   1952.   *Ad Alfonsum Calabriae ducem de principe liber*. In *Prosatori latini del Quattrocento*, edited by Eugenio Garin. Milan: R. Ricciardi.
Prinz, Wilhelm.
   1911.   *De Xenophontis Cyri Institutione*. Göttingen: Officina Academica Dieterichiana.
Proietti, Gerald.
   1987.   *Xenophon's Sparta: An Introduction*. Supplement to *Mnemosyne*, vol. 98. Leiden: Brill.
Rahe, Paul.
   1980.   "The Military Situation in Western Asia on the Eve of the Battle of Cunaxa." *American Journal of Philology* 101: 79–96.

   ———.
   1994.   *Republics Ancient and Modern*, Vol. 1. Chapel Hill: University of North Carolina Press.
Rawson, Elizabeth.
   1969.   *The Spartan Tradition in European Thought*. Oxford: Clarendon Press.
Riedinger, Jean-Claude.
   1991.   *Etude sur les Helléniques: Xénophon et l'histoire*. Paris: Les Belles Lettres.

Romilly, Jacqueline de.

1976.   "L'excuse de l'invincible amour dans la tragédie grecque." In
          Miscellanea Tragica in Honorem J. C. Kamerbeek, edited by
          J. M. Bremer, S. L. Radt, and C. J. Ruijg. Amsterdam: Hakkert.

Ruderman, Richard.

1992.   "The Rule of a Philosopher King." In *Politikos II*, edited by
          Leslie Rubin. Pittsburgh: Duquesne University Press.

Sabbadini, Remigio.

1905.   *Le scoperte dei codici latini e greci nei secole XIV e XV*.
          Florence: Sansoni.

Sage, Paula Winsor.

1994.   "Dying in Style: Xenophon's Ideal Leader and the End of the
          Cyropaedia." *Classical Journal* 90: 161–74.

Sancisi-Weerdenburg, Heleen.

1990.   "Cyrus in Italy: From Dante to Machiavelli." In *Achaemenid
          History, V: The Roots of the European Tradition*, edited by H.
          Sancisi-Weerdenburg and J. W. Drijvers. Leiden: Nederlands
          instituut voor het nabije oosten.

Scharr, Erwin.

1919.   *Xenophons Staats- und Gesellschaftsideal und seine Zeit*. Halle:
          M. Niemeyer.

Schneider, Johann Gottlob.

1815.   *Xenophontis de Cyri disciplina libri VIII*. Leipzig: Sumptibus
          hahnianae librariae.

Sidney, Sir Philip [1554–86].

1965.   *The Defense of Poesy*. Edited by Geoffrey Shepherd. London:
          T. Nelson.

Sinclair, T. A.

1967.   *A History of Greek Political Thought*. Cleveland: World.

Soulis, E. M.

1972.   *Xenophon and Thucydides*. Athens: n.p.

Spenser, Edmund [1552–99].

1965.   *The Faerie Queene*. Edited by Robert Kellogg. New York:
          Odyssey Press.

Stadter, Phillip.

1991.   "Fictional Narrative in the *Cyropaedia*." *American Journal of
          Philology* 112: 461–91.

Strauss, Leo.

1939.   "The Spirit of Sparta or the Taste of Xenophon." *Social Re-
          search* 6: 502–36.

———.

1968.   *On Tyranny: An Interpretation of Xenophon's* Hiero. Ithaca,
          N.Y.: Cornell University Press.

———.

1970. *Xenophon's Socratic Discourse: An Interpretation of the* Oeconomicus. Ithaca, N.Y.: Cornell University Press.

Swift, Jonathan.

1972. *Correspondence*, Vol. 3. Edited by Harold Williams. Oxford: Clarendon Press.

Tatum, James.

1989. *Xenophon's Imperial Fiction: On* The Education of Cyrus. Princeton, N.J.: Princeton University Press.

Tarcov, Nathan.

1982. "Quentin Skinner's Method and Machiavelli's *Prince*." *Ethics* 92: 692–709.

Too, Yun Lee.

1998. "Xenophon's *Cyropaedia*: Disfiguring the Pedagogical State." In *Pedagogy and Power. Rhetorics of Classical Learning*, edited by Yun Lee Too and Niall Livingstone. Cambridge: Cambridge University Press.

Tuplin, Christopher.

1990. "Persian Decor in *Cyropaedia*: Some Observations." In *Achaemenid History, V: The Roots of the European Tradition*, edited by H. Sancisi-Weerdenburg and J. W. Drijvers. Leiden: Nederlands instituut voor het nabije oosten.

———.

1993. *The Failings of Empire: a Reading of Xenophon*. Hellenica 2.3.11–7.5.27. Stuttgart: F. Steiner.

———.

1994. "Xenophon, Sparta and the *Cyropaedia*." In *The Shadow of Sparta*, edited by Anton Powell. London: Routledge.

Vander Waerdt, Paul A., ed.

1994. *The Socratic Movement*. Ithaca, N.Y.: Cornell University Press.

Vlastos, Gregory.

1991. *Socrates, Ironist and Moral Philosopher*. Ithaca, N.Y.: Cornell University Press.

Voigt, Georg.

1888–90. *Il risorgimento dell'antichità classica*, 2 vols. Florence: Sansoni.

Wheeler, Francis.

1962. "An Analysis of Method and Purpose in the *Cyropaedia* of Xenophon." Ph.D. diss., University of Chicago.

Willetts, Ronald.

1954. "The *Neodamodeis*." *Classical Philology* 49: 27–32.

Wood, Neal.
   1964.   "Xenophon's Theory of Leadership." *Classica et Mediaevalia* 25: 33–66.

Xenophon.
   1900–20.   *Xenophontis opera omnia*. Edited by E. C. Marchant. Oxford: Oxford Classical Library.

————.
   1968.   *Xenophontis Institutio Cyri*. Edited by W. Gemoll. Leipzig: Teubner.

General Index

Index Locorum

Compositor:	Humanist Typesetting & Graphics, Inc.
Text:	11 / 13.5 Caledonia
Display:	Caledonia
Printer and Binder:	Haddon Craftsmen